The
WITCH
of
MANSFIELD

The WITCH of MANSFIELD

The Tetched Life of Phebe Wise

MARK SEBASTIAN JORDAN

THE
History
PRESS

Published by The History Press
Charleston, SC
www.historypress.com

First published 2023

Manufactured in the United States

ISBN 9781467155212

Library of Congress Control Number: 2023937207

Extended quotations from the works of Louis Bromfield are used with the gracious permission of the Malabar Farm Foundation, which holds the copyright on Bromfield's literary works.

For Steven

CONTENTS

A NOTE FROM THE AUTHOR

As many of the sources consulted for this work are more than a century old, I have elected to keep the spelling conventions and wayward punctuation of this period in material directly quoted from these sources without correcting it—that includes both newspaper reports and the books of Louis Bromfield.

There is also another discovery that I found only after examining samples of the signature of the subject of this history. For 140 years, the press and others have given her first name as "Phoebe," the formal spelling from the source word. Today, the name is most commonly heard referring to a small, drab North American bird that makes a call that sounds like "fee bee." In Ancient Greece, the name was associated with the goddess Artemis and was used in poetry as the personification of the moon. Appropriately enough, it is also the name of a moon of Saturn that runs in a retrograde direction from the rest of the planet's moons. Yet on every sample of the woman's signature that I could find, she spelled her own name "Phebe." Therefore, I have defaulted to this spelling throughout the book, except in quoted sources that used the modernized spelling. Considering that she was still around long after seeing her name in print, she could have changed the spelling to match the world around her. In characteristic form, she didn't. I want to honor her wishes by calling her "Phebe."

Even more obscure is the word included in the title: *tetched*. It's an archaic rural word referring to someone being a little "touched," meaning "insane." Phebe Wise had a way of using it that moved the reference from insanity to a sort of eccentricity and spiritual connection with nature that might be perceived by an outsider as insanity but is, in truth, along the lines of feisty individualism. She saw this in herself and was the first to notice it in the boy who would become the world-famous writer Louis Bromfield. Bromfield spelled the word "teched" in his writings, which can be confusing in light of the modern prominence of the word *tech*, a casual abbreviation of *technology*. Therefore, I have added the "t" to keep the word as strange and distinct as it should be.

PREFACE

T he site is adjacent to one of the most visited tourist sites in Ohio, but no one comes those few steps farther aside from me. The Ohio State Reformatory looms along the ridge of Hancock Heights, balefully overlooking the small midwestern city of Mansfield in such a shockingly vivid way that it has become a movie star in its own right. Featured in several films—but most unforgettably as the titular prison in the classic 1993 film *The Shawshank Redemption*—the reformatory is now visited by hundreds of thousands of tourists every year.

Few of them know that the prison was built on property sold to the State of Ohio by Christian Wise, the father of the subject of this book. The imposing façade of the massive building was carved out of the stone from the old quarry across the road, making the place seem to rise out of the ground. Just beyond the prison's overflow parking lot stands a spring-fed pond. Nothing marks the site, but I like to visit there today and reflect that this pond played a significant role in launching the trajectory of a child who became a Pulitzer Prize–winning author.

Today, the hillside is overgrown with impassible brambles. When it used to be mowed, I would sometimes walk up the hillside above the spring, which has, for years, been the right-of-way for large wooden telephone poles with a swath of electric lines departing the substation on top of the ridge. I would envision what used to stand there: a couple of small barns, a toolshed, a chicken coop, and a small farmhouse that once held a square grand piano, ancient ball gowns, hundreds if not thousands of books, and a pet horse. As I approached the small, leveled-off grade where the house once stood, I was able to see the rectangular shape of the house in the pattern of spring daffodils, planted long ago. Off to the side was a full patch of daffodils, remnants of the garden that once covered most of the hillside. One wonders if they are still coming up every spring or have been choked off by thorns.

It wasn't long after I first heard about Ceely Rose, the infamous poisoner of Malabar Farm, that I heard about Phebe Wise. During my childhood, growing up just north of Mansfield, the newspaper ran a column of local history stories compiled by Virgil Stanfield. I became a fan of this column because Stanfield was, at heart, a storyteller, and his curation of stories from the past for readers of his own day thrilled me. Here were almost-forgotten stories being rescued from oblivion and saved for the future. It struck me as a kind of magic that a good storyteller could suggest images that brought long-dead characters back to life in the reader's imagination to walk once again whenever the words are spoken or read.

Phebe Wise was one of Stanfield's favorites. The time I first encountered Stanfield's writings, the early 1980s, was only fifty years after Wise's death. Thus, living memory still held Phebe as the queen of Mansfield's outsiders, a woman so eccentric that some thought she was literally a witch. She loomed large in the story of Mansfield's most famous writer, Louis Bromfield, and through him had become known around the world. I was fascinated.

I was amazed by Phebe's story, not least because it showed Mansfield tolerating a highly eccentric individual. If there was one thing that my reading and observations of American pop culture via television told me in my youth, it was that society was not kind to those who stood outside the mainstream. Thousands of tales have been told about how the nail that sticks out gets hammered down. I wondered: what was it about Phebe—about Mansfield—that proved an exception?

It was only as the years went by that I began to understand how much Phebe's story resonated with me on a personal level. After first researching the Ceely Rose case, I wrote a drama about her story that we eventually produced at Malabar Farm State Park. Even as I was launching that project, I knew that there another story that had profound connections to Malabar, and that was the story of Phebe Wise's many misadventures. To the best of my knowledge, Phebe Wise never stepped foot into Richland County's Pleasant Valley, where Malabar is located. But Malabar Farm wouldn't exist if it weren't for her, because she was the first person who pointed out that there was something special, something otherworldly about the young Lewis Brumfield, who would later become world-famous writer and conservationist Louis Bromfield. And if Louis Bromfield had never existed, I hardly think I'd be here writing this, as his example was what proved to me that even a kid from a working-class family in Mansfield, Ohio, could become a writer.

But it runs deeper than that, too. Growing up as a closeted kid in rural Ohio, just outside of Mansfield, I knew I was an outsider. On some level, I was drawn to Phebe Wise, because she, too, was a stubborn outsider following her vision instead of the stilted rules of a society that didn't leave wiggle room for nonconformists. In 2004, I wrote my play about Phebe Wise, whom I still knew at the time as "Phoebe," as the second part of my Malabar Trilogy. Louis Bromfield himself came last in the trilogy. I realized that I had written *Ceely* for the people whom I had grown up with in Ohio. I wrote *Louie* for posterity. I wrote *Phoebe* for myself.

Phebe Wise was, above all things, a philosopher. She had a distinctive way of looking at the world, one that was spiritual and nature-based in a way that was decades ahead of its time. Louis Bromfield could take those wings and fly. Another young Mansfielder, Jake Kastanowitz, would fly too high, too quick, and plummet like Icarus.

Phebe's story is interwoven with tragedy, politics, violence, philosophy, comedy, and mystery. Against the odds, she lived as an independent woman in an age when women were expected to marry and raise children. At the very least, a woman was expected to defer to men. Phebe Wise would have none of that. For better or worse, she was intent on being whoever she wanted to be, whether that meant cutting her hair short and dressing in men's clothes, strutting the streets of downtown Mansfield in an ancient ball gown, playing a forbidden banjo or letting her pet horse traipse through the house.

Was she insane? I don't think so. More likely, she was crazy like a fox as the rural idiom goes. There was tremendous cleverness behind Phebe's wayward behaviors, an intelligence that makes what she did understandable as a coping mechanism, as a diversion, as an expression of her individuality.

After Louis Bromfield achieved world fame, his publishers were always amused at his instructions for the first printing: a handful of copies were to be sent to the author, several copies were assigned to be sent to all the most important literary critics and one copy was to be sent to Miss Phebe Wise, Olivesburg Road, Mansfield, Ohio.

Standing on the hillside where Phebe once stood, as the connection between our mundane world and the greater, more elusive realm of the energy simmers just beneath the skin of reality, I can feel her influence animating what I do, today, ninety years after her death.

It's a proud and strange legacy that propels me onward, one that I wish to share with all those other tetched people out there who are seeking substance in a world addicted to flash and noise.

Mark Sebastian Jordan
Mansfield, Ohio
March 2023

ACKNOWLEDGEMENTS

The author wishes to thank Boyd Addlesperger, Louis Andres, Tom Bachelder, Stephanie Bowman, Daniel J. Feiertag, Gina Jessee, Michelle Jordan-Frias, Timothy McKee, Mary McKinley, Rebecca McKinney, Brett Mitchell, Lori Morey, Elizabeth Couch Nordstrom, Sunda Peters, and Paul Smith for their invaluable help.

Special thanks to the following institutions: Malabar Farm State Park, the Malabar Farm Foundation, the John Sherman Local History and Genealogy Room at the Mansfield Richland County Public Library, the Ohio State Reformatory, the Ohio Genealogical Society, and the Richland County Probate Court Archives.

Valued personal assistance came from Rudy Braden, Mandy Breitenbucher, Theresa Gardner, Bryan Gladden, Lucas Hargis, Victoria Hoefler, Lloyd and Violet Jordan, Phillip and Lisa Jordan, Wayne and Veena Jordan, Tabitha Payne Kennedy, Atohi Nelson, Nancy Nixon, Jill and Andrew Poloni, Glenn Stackhouse, Mark Sylvanus Stark, Raven Starr, and Andrea Wittmer.

The author is thankful for the valuable idea sounding from Mason Boor, Danny Brown, Melanie Collopy, Katy Davis, David FitzSimmons, Timothy Gorka, Don Hilton, Phillip Jordan, Marilyn Kousoulas, Ann Laudeman, Steve McQuown, Alison Stine, Michelle Kin Stoneburner, Annie Tarpley, and Kerry Trautman and the Redditors at r/whatisthisthing and r/century homes for discussing the quirks and uses of peculiar turrets on old houses.

1

AN INTOLERABLE SITUATION

S
he could take it no longer.

For almost ten years, Phebe Wise had been putting up with the ever more demanding attentions of her self-styled suitor Jake Kastanowitz. At first, Phebe had been amused by the young factory worker, who lived just a block away in Polacktown, one of Mansfield's working-class neighborhoods.

Jake thought Phebe was the height of class and money, and compared to his family, she was. The daughter of a prominent teacher, preacher, and founding father of the Ohio town, Phebe was smart, and she cut a striking figure on the streets of Mansfield. After her parents were gone and she inherited their house and money, she began breaking out the old ball gowns her mother kept in the attic, gowns dating to the Civil War and earlier, for special occasions. Phebe began wearing the gowns when she walked to town, letting the dresses' trains drag along in the dirt. She didn't care. They were her dresses now, and she could use them however she damn well pleased.

Jake watched her walk past. He was poor, typical of the eastern European immigrants who settled Polacktown and other working neighborhoods in order to receive the gift of working long, dirty hours in the factories of the Flats. Despite his poverty, Jakob Kastanowitz was smart. He spoke seven languages and read literature. He aspired to greatness in the world.

Phebe became more intrigued by the intense young man as she gradually discerned how smart he was. When, one day, he heard her playing her old square piano—the instrument first carted over the Appalachians to Mansfield from Baltimore, according to local lore—Jake asked what she was playing. Phebe told him that it was a piece written by Beethoven. Jake asked for more. Over the next few weeks, she began teaching him the classics by shouting out through the open window what she was about to play, and Jake, in return, shouted back from the front yard which pieces he wanted to hear again. At heart, Phebe was always a teacher.

But Jake wanted more than an education. He wanted to be a part of society. He wanted to have the money to live on his own with a house and property—like Phebe. He wanted to have an educated society woman as his partner, his equal. He wanted to claim someone smart and beautiful as his own. He wanted Phebe Wise.

He told her so. Phebe was alarmed. All she could think of were the two things her father kept warning her about over and over again as the years ticked by before he died. First, the spring on their property made the land valuable, and men would try to swindle it away from her. And second, plainly: "No man will ever want an Indian-looking girl like you."

She rebuked Jake and stopped talking to him. He started coming up to her porch and looking into her windows. When he saw her, he would try to give her the gift of music, singing songs to her in a voice that grew louder and uglier as the years went by and his desperation grew. When she told him to get off her property, he would hide in the hedge out front, which didn't conceal him at all. He would mail her letters that, over time, grew more and more suggestive. One day, she was startled when she walked around the corner and found Jake standing in her living room, recklessly grinning. She chased him off and reminded him she owned a gun. There were times when she had to hit him with a fire poker to stop his advances, and there were other times when she bodily threw him out of her yard onto the road.

Slowly but steadily, Jake's behavior escalated. He told Phebe that he would continue to court her until she agreed to be his wife and that nothing would stop that from happening. When she pulled her curtains shut to block his view, he brought a hand drill from home and bored small holes in her window frames. Using a stiff wire, he pushed aside the curtain until he could catch sight of her and burst into song. Phebe learned to keep her doors locked and blocked, else the young man would come inside.

Jake began missing work so he could station himself before Phebe's house and watch her every move. When she complained to the city police, they began arresting him for disorderly conduct and throwing him in jail for the weekend. Upon his release on Monday morning, he'd make a beeline for Phebe's home. He stopped going to work and lost his job at the Baxter Stove Company. Jake was found incapable of standing trial due to his increasingly unstable mental condition, so he was sent off to the Toledo State Hospital for treatment.

In Toledo, Jake settled down and demonstrated his intelligence to the staff, and he explained his irresponsible behavior away as the result of unrequited love. The doctors decided after a few months that Jakob Kastanowitz had stabilized, and they sent him home. He immediately made a beeline over to Phebe's house.

His letters to Phebe began to include outrageous drawings of the things he wanted to do to her, which brought a felony charge against him for sending obscene matter through the mail. That move earned him a stay in the Canton Workhouse. But none of it made much of an impact on him. Once released, he'd head to Phebe's.

The cycle continued: Jake smiling while he was being arrested and then getting thrown in jail overnight for being a nuisance. Then he'd continue to harass Phebe, trying to spy on her, bursting into crazed song and attempting to break into her house. He told her that she would become his wife—or else. He would make sure that no one else would have her. It was intolerable.

One morning, when the coast was clear, Phebe stalked down to the trolley tracks at the bottom of the hill and flagged down car no. 20, the one that always ran the line from downtown out to the Ohio State Reformatory, the intermediate penitentiary that loomed on the hill beyond Phebe's house. She stepped aboard without offering to pay and sat down. The conductors had given up trying to get her to pay and simply took it as a matter of course Phebe Wise rode for free.

Phebe left the trolley downtown and marched across the square to the Richland County Jail. She stormed into the office of Sheriff James Boals and informed him that he was having a meeting with her. By this point, like most in Mansfield, Sheriff Boals knew better than to try to put Phebe in her place, so he set his other business aside and listened. He knew the case well but also knew that the current regulations tied his hands. There were no laws in the books at that time that addressed suitors who became obsessed with their intended mates, and he had no grounds on which to hold Kastanowitz for more than a night or so in jail.

"Isn't there anything you can do?" Phebe asked, at the end of her patience.

The sheriff explained that as the laws currently stood, his answer was no.

"This is going to end one of two ways, Phebe," Sheriff Boals said. "Either you marry him, or you shoot him."

She didn't marry him.

2

A TRADITION OF STRANGENESS

The Ohio Territory was the first part of the vast Northwest Territory to be settled, starting as early as the 1700s. The influx of homesteaders began even before the American Revolution wound down. This rapid and reckless expansion was stalled in the 1780s by strategic raids committed by Native groups who crossed the Ohio River and harassed white settlements in what was then Virginia (modern-day West Virginia). The local militia's response was the infamously horrific Gnadenhutten Massacre, in which peaceful American Natives were murdered as part of a supposed deterrent. Instead, it stoked a thirst for revenge.

With continuing border hostilities, General George Washington sought to neutralize the threat. He called on his retiring western land agent Colonel William Crawford to lead one last expedition west in 1782 to strike Native settlements on the upper part of the Sandusky River. This militia army clumsily made their way across the frontier, rarely spotting any Natives, which should have told them something. They were being tracked the entire way. They camped at a spring on the edge of the plateau that marks the beginning of the central highlands of north-central Ohio, a place known today as Springmill on the north side of what is now Mansfield. The group continued a little farther west and found the Native villages abandoned. Just as the commanders were about to turn back, a combined force of Natives and British regulars surrounded them. The militia escaped with heavy losses that night, including the capture and subsequent torture and immolation of Colonel Crawford. That event cast a long shadow over north-central Ohio—from then to now—where the war crime is commemorated in the names of local counties, towns, and schools.

Native wars flared across the region for the next dozen years, until U.S. forces, under Major General "Mad Anthony" Wayne, defeated a confederacy of Native forces led by Blue Jacket at the Battle of Fallen Timbers in 1794. The subsequent Treaty of Greenville drew an angled line across Ohio, giving the southeastern two-thirds of the state to U.S. settlers, while Natives were granted the northwestern third of the state, supposedly in perpetuity. As the state of Ohio was organized in the following years, Richland County became the keystone of the north-central part of the state, with the central highlands cutting through the middle of the county. Almost the entire county sat north of the Greenville Treaty line, making it, by law, Native territory.

It didn't take long for violations of the treaty to begin. White settlers pushed north of the line, and the remaining Wyandot and Lenape tribes were gathered onto reservations near the spot where Crawford was executed in what became Wyandot County. In Richland, small settlements were established as pioneers pushed northward through the Appalachian foothills. On the last ridge before the beginning of the rolling plains of northwest Ohio, a community was established in 1808, the year the Greenville Treaty was officially revoked. Named after U.S. Surveyor General Jared Mansfield, the community grew slowly.

JOHNNY APPLESEED.

Entrepreneur and mystic John Chapman, better known as Johnny Appleseed, set the tone for Mansfield's tolerance of eccentrics. *John Sherman Room, Mansfield Richland County Public Library.*

During the War of 1812, blockhouses were built to serve as shelters from the hostilities. It's around this period that Mansfield's first engagement with a notable eccentric began. John Chapman was an entrepreneur from Massachusetts who traveled the Ohio frontier planting apple trees and then bartering with seeds from his orchards. Apples were highly desired fruits on the frontier, providing attractive flavor and needed nourishment. They were also great for making cider and the fermented drink applejack. A drink like applejack was favored because of the relative safety of alcohol, which killed off any biological contaminants that could be present in groundwater.

Chapman purchased land along the frontier and planted extensive orchards across the region. He would then harvest seeds and travel across the state, selling and bartering the seeds. This would have been a labor-intensive activity for anyone, but Chapman was moved by his spiritual beliefs to give himself additional challenges. He traveled on foot—barefoot, no less—carrying his seeds and the few possessions he needed. He grew accustomed to sleeping outside, and in time, he grew to immensely prefer it, rejecting offers to sleep in settlers' houses. Legend has it that he wore his metal saucepan as a hat and shield against rain. Remarkably, he was known to travel in all seasons and all weather.

Due to his association with the wares he sold, Chapman became widely known as Johnny Appleseed. Ohio, like any frontier, was a collection of people challenged with establishing communities and surviving. This meant that little time was left for judging the conformity of other people, which benefitted eccentrics like Johnny Appleseed. As the years went by and the seed seller found Ohio's early residents either indifferent to or amused by his individuality, he stepped more fully into the role of the local eccentric.

A significant part of Chapman's motivation to be on the frontier was not business at all, though by all accounts, he was a highly successful businessman. The fact that he saw himself as a voice of faith in the wilderness is plain. An ardent Swedenborgian Christian, Chapman also took printed pamphlets with him on his travels and arranged to have more sent to him in various locations. A mystic accustomed to spending long hours alone, Chapman made spiritual proselytization a key part of his life. Selling seeds was his trade, but saving souls was his mission. Part of that came through handing out tracts, but he also led by example, even becoming so intent on being nondestructive that it is said he would camp without a fire in order to avoid burning insects attracted by the light.

Johnny Appleseed made Mansfield one of his bases of operation, finding the residents tolerant of his unusual lifestyle and increasingly peculiar discourse. He was known to partake in the social life of the fledgling town at times. On one occasion, a traveling preacher was pontificating to a crowd on the village's square about the lack of humble believers on the frontier.

"Where is the barefoot Christian?" the pompous preacher asked rhetorically. Unexpectedly, a loud cackling rose up from the back of the crowd, and a pair of bare feet could be seen sticking up in the air.

"Here I am, reverend!" shouted Johnny Appleseed, who had been reclining on a woodpile before he leaned back and stuck his well-traveled feet in the air to mock the pompous preacher.

When the War of 1812 broke out, Chapman centered his activities on Mansfield, which was safer than points farther northwest, which were subject to attack from the British, who had seized Detroit. But when British agitation of Native allies led to several attacks in north-central Ohio, Chapman made a dramatic twenty-four-mile run to the village of Mount Vernon in Knox County for reinforcements. This move stabilized the situation in Richland County and made the eccentric a local hero.

Mansfield's tolerance for peculiar people was extended to an early itinerant musician. Orrin Pharris would travel town to town, from Norwalk to Newark, playing for barn dances, formal balls, and other social occasions. He was taken to heart by these communities as one of Ohio's treasures, no matter how eccentric he became.

According to surviving accounts, Orrin Pharris was born in New York around 1790. He made his way to Ohio around 1815, making him one of the early settlers of the area, considering that Mansfield wasn't even officially platted as a village until the 1820s. In his early years, Pharris was perceived by his fellow pioneers as a reasonably normal person, a tailor who loved playing music in his spare time. He was known for being good-looking, well dressed, musical, and unmarried, though one source claims that in his early years in Ohio, Pharris declared his love for a young woman in Newark.

According to a *Mansfield Semi-Weekly News* reminiscence from 1899 written by Mathias Day, Pharris lived and played music for a spell at Cully's Hotel in Newark. He fell in love with a local young lady, but she did not return his interest. His brooding over this rejection began the process of unbalancing young Orrin's mind, which gradually accelerated over the years. It isn't known if the story had true roots or was merely concocted as a way to explain away Pharris's long-standing lack of interest in women.

The fiddler was known to be talkative in his younger years, sometimes running on at great length on subjects that caught his interest, but he always talked with such pleasant charm that people accepted it as part of his ebullient personality. His playing was praised extensively by those in the know. One listener, quoted by A.J. Baughman in his *History of Richland County* in 1908, compared him to the most famous concert violinist of the day, the world-touring master Ole Bull from Norway: "Ole Bull could not draw a smoother bow, nor produce sweeter melody upon the violin than did Orrin Pharris."

Since he was playing in the early 1800s, Pharris's dance repertory likely consisted of schottisches and reels. It's unlikely he would have played waltzes, as the waltz craze was just firing up in Europe in the 1820s and would not yet have reached rural Ohio. When not playing dances, he played hymns. Mathias Day's written recollections said that "his hymns were always sung as if his soul went out in them." Such an expressive musician was much in demand.

But Pharris met with disaster at a dance in Granville in Licking County in 1832. A young man by the name of Cuppy, the son of a prominent Newark landlord, had been pounding down alcohol all evening. He then grabbed an attractive girl and drunkenly informed her that she was going to dance with him. The girl was terrified of Cuppy's aggression, but he would not relent. The crowd of dancers around them dropped silent.

Cuppy shouted at Orrin Pharris to play them a fiddle tune so they could dance. Pharris was appalled at the youth's behavior. The musician stood silently, avoiding eye contact with the belligerent drunk. Even after the young man threatened him, the fiddler would not raise his bow. Suddenly, Cuppy grabbed a bottle of liquor and poured it all over Pharris's hair and beard.

"I will set that on fire if you don't play!" Cuppy bellowed.

Pharris silently refused. Cuppy grabbed a candle and set the fiddler's hair on fire before anyone could stop him. Other partygoers saved Pharris's life by quenching the flames, but the burns were extensive. Pharris's recovery took a long time, and it left him permanently disfigured. Though he continued playing, Pharris very rarely spoke for the rest of his life, brooding over his misfortune. He eventually stopped working completely and turned to drink and begging. Only music kept him tied to this world. He would travel throughout the area, playing for food and a place to sleep. If he encountered a stray kitten, he would carry it in his coat as he traveled.

In his later years, he could often be seen walking the streets of area towns, playing the fiddle and singing in a fine tenor voice. Groups of boys would follow him, taunting him until he either played a tune for them or raised his walking stick and shouted at them, "Go off, you varmints!" If he had his cat with him, he'd threaten to "set this Bengal tiger on you" as well, suggesting he retained a sense of humor, even after all his misfortune.

Around 1860, he trekked to Shelby, north of Mansfield, to play at an event. He collapsed that evening, and lacking a better place to take him, the doctor who was summoned took Pharris to the Richland County Infirmary on Olivesburg Road. It was there that he was recorded in the 1860 census,

Orrin Pharris.

Itinerant fiddler Orrin Pharris upped the ante for Mansfield's experience of eccentrics. *John Sherman Room, Mansfield Richland County Public Library.*

described as "insane." It wasn't long before he was stricken by a further attack. Orrin Pharris's alleged last words were a quote from his favorite hymn, "Take and save a trembling sinner, Lord." He was buried in an unmarked grave in the indigent patient's cemetery.

Having dealt with fascinating eccentrics like Johnny Appleseed and Orrin Pharris, Mansfield was primed for the appearance of Phebe Wise.

3

PIONEERS OF MANSFIELD

T he first cabin of what was to become Mansfield was built in 1808 by Jacob Newman, but the actual formation of the community took place over many years. One of the last people to arrive in Richland County who was still called a founding father was Reverend Christian Wise, who arrived in 1833.

Documentation about Wise is surprisingly elusive, considering his obvious wealth and education. Even the earliest histories of the county fail to identify precise information about his childhood, other than to say that he was from Baltimore, Maryland, and that his father was a physician and surgeon and a master of five languages. Such a prominent and successful person ought to be identifiable, but the problem that quickly arises is that early records of the colony—and, subsequently, the state—of Maryland are incomplete and likely weren't extensive in the first place.

Compounding that difficulty is the fact that Wise was a common name in Baltimore. Some people of that name were of British ancestry, but it was also a common Anglicization of the German name Weiss, and the given name Christian is certainly far more common in the German tradition than it is in the British. Christian Wise's father may have been prominent in the late 1700s and early 1800s, but his son's separation seems to have been so thorough that the connection is now lost. While it is speculation to take that as a possible hint at discord between Wise and his father, there is nothing in Wise's later relationship with his youngest daughter to dissuade the notion that he might have been an exceedingly difficult man.

Reverend Christian Wise and his wife, Julia, Phebe's parents. *John Sherman Room, Mansfield/Richland County Public Library.*

Wise is said to have been educated at Hanover and Brighton Colleges in his youth, though records for any such schools in the Baltimore area are lacking. There is a Hanover College in Indiana, which dates to the early years of the frontier, but it lacks any record of a Christian Wise attending in its early years. If the Baltimore Wises were sufficiently wealthy, these schools could have been anywhere in the existing United States or even in England.

At some point, Christian Wise met Julia Ann Riegel from Broadbecks in York County, Pennsylvania, just over the Maryland border. Julia Ann was the daughter of a family who had moved from the Palatinate in Rheinland-Pfalz, Germany, to southeastern Pennsylvania in the 1700s. The Riegels lived in Brodbecks in York County. Ludwig (later Americanized to Lewis) Riegel married Susanna Eppley in 1788, and they had Julia Ann in 1810. It isn't known how Julia Ann met Christian Wise, but the areas where each lived are not a great distance apart. And since one source says that Julia Ann was a schoolteacher, she and Christian may have shared an interest in education. They married in the late 1820s or early 1830s and headed west to the Ohio countryside in 1833.

Wise apparently first bought a tract of land on the north side of Mansfield "on the state road," today's Ohio State Route 13. But looking across the way,

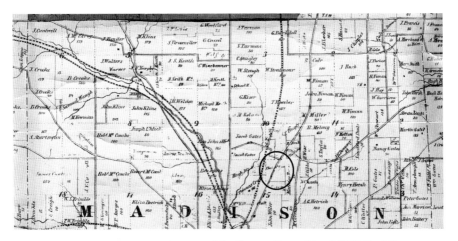

The Wise property on an 1856 plat map. *John Sherman Room, Mansfield Richland County Public Library.*

he must have fancied the fine hillside in his view, as he sold the first property and purchased fifty-eight acres of land on Olivesburg Road, just a little east of the first property. This new property was located on Quarry Hill, the hill overlooking the north side of Mansfield, and included one of the quarries on the ridge. In addition to farming this land, Wise served as an educator at a local establishment known as "The University" and taught in several public schoolhouses. A.J. Baughman's 1908 *History of Richland County, Ohio*, states that Wise "did much to advance the intellectual status of the community in the early days, and many of the now prominent men of the community were among his pupils." He was also elected as Richland County's first county surveyor, a position he served in for twenty years.

Christian Wise's prominence in Mansfield society is suggested by his known friendships with prominent political figures, including John Sherman. Sherman, the brother of legendary U.S. Civil War general William Tecumseh Sherman, was to become a prominent U.S. senator and the sponsor of the important Sherman Anti-Trust Act in 1890. Sherman remained Mansfield-based despite his frequent presence in Washington, D.C. He lived in a mansion on Mansfield's Park Avenue West. The northern end of Sherman's property contained an apple orchard bordered by Third Street. Living just across the street from the orchard—and frequently raiding it—was a young Louis Bromfield, the Mansfield-born writer who later made Phebe Wise world-famous.

Wise was said to be a staunch Jeffersonian Democrat, and he attained the status of third-degree bishop in the Dunkard Church, where he preached for forty years. According to Baughman, Wise's long term as county surveyor brought him into wide contact with the local populace. "In pioneer days his circle of friends embraced almost every resident of this portion of the state, and through the years he had enjoyed the warm regard and confidence of all with whom he was associated, being highly esteemed for his many excellent qualities."

A testimony to his reputation can be found in an 1844 Mansfield newspaper, which advertises a piece of land for sale "as numbered on a plat by Christian Wise, county surveyor," as if that is a mark of integrity. It became a standard phrase of quality in Richland County land transactions for the next quarter century. Baughman's profile confirms Wise's reputation, adding that Wise kept in touch with the advanced thought and progress of the day: "He was broad minded and progressive in his views, at all times exemplifying the humanitarian spirit which was one of his salient characteristics."

When the Civil War loomed in 1861, Christian Wise's neighbors to the north, the Tingley family, sold acreage to the State of Ohio for the creation of an army training ground. Camp Mordecai Bartley opened that summer and was in operation for the next two years.

After the war, the state began looking for a site for a future intermediary penitentiary, a facility created to separate young, first-time offenders from the career criminals housed in the Ohio Penitentiary in Columbus. Already holding the former Tingley acreage from Camp Bartley, the state approached Christian Wise about buying part of his acreage for the new prison. He agreed to sell dozens of acres of his land, limiting the area so that he did not turn over the large spring that stood just downhill from his house. The front grounds of the prison, as well as the main building itself, were built on the former Wise land.

Wise also agreed to supply stone for the foundation and facing of the facility from the quarry that existed on the eastern side of his property, east of Olivesburg Road. This now-unused quarry remains in place. The construction of the new Ohio State Reformatory began in 1886, but the prison did not reach opening condition until 1896, with the official completion of the 250,000-square-foot building not achieved until 1910.

The prison was not the only thing being constructed along the hillside that had become known as Hancock Heights. A neighborhood of brick houses had been built for the workers who were constructing the reformatory. Christian Wise agreed to sell an acre at the intersection of Olivesburg and Fleming Falls Roads to be used to build Excelsior School (later known as Hancock Heights

Spring on the Wise property. *Author's collection.*

School) to serve the neighborhood. It is likely Wise taught there for a time, as at least two of his children later would.

Around the same time, as the railroads and small factories began spreading up the hills from the industrial Flats area on the north side of Mansfield, a new neighborhood was built at the intersection of Olivesburg Road and Longview Avenue also on land that had once belonged to Wise. Fairview was built to provide low-cost housing for the eastern European immigrants who were coming to Mansfield for factory work. It soon was nicknamed "Polacktown" by Mansfield residents.

It was to loom large in Phebe Wise's future.

4

FROM STUDENT TO TEACHER TO CARETAKER

R everend Wise's wife, Julia Ann, gave birth to ten children during their years in Mansfield, though two of them died in childhood, and three more died before the end of the century. By that time, only five children remained: Frank, Ella, Mary, William, and Phebe.

There may have been another Phebe Wise first. This girl was born to another Wise family—it is unknown whether they were related—led by David Wise. This Phebe was born in 1847 or 1848 and died in 1850 of dysentery, according to local death records. If David Wise was related, Christian may have named his daughter in honor of the lost cousin, though it would seem such a maneuver might cause family tension. It could also be a complete coincidence. But this suggests that Christian's Phebe was born sometime between 1848 and 1852, making her considerably younger than the legends later portrayed her. While she later appeared to demur about her age, some sources claim that she admitted she didn't actually know her exact age. That's an unexpected situation for a woman who was clearly highly educated. The 1850 census gives Phebe's age as two, while the 1880 census suggests a birth date as early as 1846.

Phebe benefitted from her father's progressive ideals, as young women of the nineteenth century were often not given extensive educations. The expected social role of women in this period was to marry and raise children. But in accordance with Reverend Wise's views, Phebe was given a thorough education, which included training in music. Phebe was known to have been proficient in playing the piano as well as the banjo.

A production photograph from the historical drama *Phoebe*, showing Phebe Wise (played by Chevy Troxell Bond) with her banjo. *Author's collection.*

And it is here that we encounter the darker side of Christian Wise's gleaming public reputation. While he was identified as progressive and in touch with modern thought, there were apparently limits to Wise's forward thinking. While he approved of Phebe's playing the piano, performing proper European classics, such as Beethoven and Mozart, he was angered by her taste for the banjo, according to a delightfully gossipy—if highly wayward—account written by Marji Hazen for the *Mansfield News Journal* in 1965.

Wise regarded the banjo, a folk instrument with African roots, as a tool for inferior music—or, as he termed it, "devil music." Hazen said that Phebe taunted her father by questioning why, if the Black Americans were so supposedly inferior, did they have the best tunes? But Phebe knew she could only rebel against her father's stern control so far. She took to playing only the piano if she knew her father was around and breaking out the banjo only when she knew he was safely out of the house.

There is only one grainy photograph of the house in which the Wises lived. For a wealthy family who had—or at least attempted to have—ten children, the house appears tiny. It was a typical one-and-a-half-story farmhouse from the pre–Civil War era. It appears from the photograph that the house faced westward, away from Olivesburg Road (today's Wayne Street, Ohio State Route 545), looking out over the flat farmlands north of Mansfield—the same view that would later give the adjacent housing development of Fairview its name. The growing town of Mansfield would have been visible, rising on the next hill to the south, from the industrial Flats neighborhood (also known as Frogtown thanks to its frequent flooding) in the valley between the two hills.

The original farmhouse, built by Christian Wise in the 1830s, would have had a square footprint. A one-story addition extended the north side of the house, giving the building a rectangular footprint. A chimney can be seen jutting out of the main section of the house, with a separate chimney likely built for a kitchen in the addition. In the 1933 photograph taken following

The only known photograph of the Wise house. *Ohio Department of Natural Resources, Malabar Farm State Park.*

Phebe's death, the gutters are beginning to fall off the addition. The house sat empty for a short period before it was demolished.

What was confusing about the house is that there was some sort of structure in front of the join of the original house and the addition that looks like a tower or cupola. Though the quality of the photograph is poor, it looks as if the cupola sat in front of the main section at the end of the porch. It matches writer Louis Bromfield's later description of the house having a tiny turret.

Genealogist Marji Hazen described the house vividly in a 1965 article for the *Mansfield News Journal*: "The house had originally been a log cabin. Old Wise had built the rambling additions from salvaged, secondhand lumber, and made rafters of tree limbs—not any two of which would have measured the same angle."

The upstairs bedrooms would have been small, and it would have been unlikely to have more than two small bedrooms, which seems impossibly small for a large family. But an inspection of the original property confirms the impression. The house was located on the hillside sweeping down from Hancock Heights on the west side of Olivesburg Road. Today, this parcel of land is a state right-of-way for utility lines, and the house is long gone. The property's prominent spring is still visible down the hill, but only two clues identify the house's location. One is that about two-thirds of the way up the hillside and slightly toward the south side of the right-of-way, there is a small leveled-off piece of ground. From the bottom of the hill, the flattened area is almost impossible to see, but it is more evident when walking up through the field. Alas, today, the hillside is so overgrown, it would be challenging to cross it without a machete.

In 2017, it was possible to explore the hillside after it had been mowed by the state. Noticeable at that time was the vague shape of a rectangle formed by daffodils that were originally planted by either Phebe Wise herself or her mother, Julia Ann. They briefly gave a clear reference for the size of the house—and it was not large. Those flowers were accompanied by another patch of flowers outlining part of Phebe's garden, which later grew to overtake the entire hillside. As of this writing, it is unknown whether any of the flowers have survived the sprawling brambles that now cover the site.

The house must have had a beautiful view, but a houseful of children with a strong-minded father must have fueled incredible tension at times. It may have been in those years of youthful tension that Phebe first began retreating into nature and developing her extraordinary connection with nature that Bromfield later described. In addition to extensive farm fields on the north side of Mansfield, there were also several surviving patches of woods in the area, which would have given Phebe places for contemplative retreat.

Whatever tensions may have arisen, Christian Wise made sure that his children had thorough educations. One of Phebe's brothers, Frank, was even sent to the Vermillion Institute in the town of Vermillion in Ashland County,

The former location of the Wise home today. *Author's collection.*

today known as Hayesville. Two of Phebe's siblings became professors, and two others became primary school teachers. Phebe herself was so bright that by the age of fourteen, she began teaching school at various one-room schoolhouses in the area.

As the years passed, it became clear that Phebe, as the youngest child, would become the caretaker of her aging parents. That was the customary role of youngest daughter in rural American society at this time, so it came as no surprise. The reward to the caretaker was that she would later inherit the property after her parents passed, and that was the acknowledged plan in this case.

What is surprising, though, is how much Christian Wise did to ensure Phebe remained single. Accounts claim that Wise continually undercut any romantic aspirations his daughter might ever have had by telling her that after she inherited the property, men would come calling on her with the intention of marrying her. But he warned her that they wouldn't be after her. They'd be willing to wed her in order to get control of the high-quality spring on the Wise property, which he believed was the finest-quality water in the area. He told Phebe men wouldn't want her—they'd be after the valuable property.

"No one would ever want an Indian-looking girl like you," Wise was alleged to have said.

If this is true, it's an extraordinary comment for a father to make to his teenaged daughter. The sourcing of the comment remains hazy but persistent. It fueled the supposition that Phebe was, in fact, not Christian and Julia Ann's daughter but an adopted Native baby. On the surface, that might appear highly unlikely, but it is true that the last contingent of Lenape (called the Delaware tribe by white settlers) did not leave Ohio until the mid-1800s. There were a handful of Natives who chose not to move west and instead did their best to live alongside the white settlers. One such lingerer was a Delaware Native associated with parts of Knox County, just south of the Richland County border.

Big Jelloway Creek took its name from the Native chieftain who still lived in the area when the settlers arrived. The settlers called him Chief Tom Jelloway, but the meaning of his Native name isn't known—nor is any of his substantial history. He was known to be one of the chiefs of the Delaware (Lenape) tribe.

According to the 1881 *History of Knox County*, Tom Jelloway lived in Butler Township of Knox County, though he hunted all over the area. Jelloway was said to be fond of the white settlers' fashion and would dress like them, occasionally selling handmade trinkets to the settlers in order to get some legal tender to buy clothes.

Jelloway also identified himself as a bird charmer. A settler by the name of Beatty didn't believe the old Native and challenged him to prove it. Jelloway immediately climbed into a large cherry tree on Beatty's property and began chanting a series of strange vocal calls. Instantly, birds began flocking to the upper branches of the tree, some landing on Jelloway's shoulders and head as he smiled down at Beatty.

The only other piece of biographical information known about Chief Tom Jelloway is that he declined to move west to reservations with the rest of his tribe. He lived out his life in Knox County, having friendly relations with the newcomers. Though Jelloway's death isn't documented, it is worth pointing out that the final western removal of the last of the Native tribes from Ohio didn't take place until 1843.

Could a handful of Natives have handed off a child to a local preacher before leaving the area? It's certainly possible that a Native infant—or even more likely, a multiracial baby—might have been adopted out. And the uncertainty about Phebe's age would seem to support such murky beginnings. But Bromfield dismissed the idea, claiming that it was a mangled version of the truth, which was that Phebe's family had some Delaware blood deep in their history, like so many other frontier families. Bromfield, however, offers no source other than the family stories of his youth.

A gossipy newspaper history by Marji Hazen, published decades after Phebe's death, capitalizes on the rumor with an exaggerated description of the woman:

> *No one remembers Phoebe Wise as a young girl. Grandfathers say that she was considered beautiful by their grandfathers. No one knows for sure whether she was really old Wise's daughter or whether he brought her home to raise with his own four children after Indians abandoned her as they were departing out of Mohican country to wander into oblivion to the west. She looked like an Indian. No one will deny that. She had snapping black eyes, coarse dark hair, and skin the color of copper.*

Even Bromfield attributed Phebe's dark hair, "black as a crow's wing," to her Native ancestry.

Hazen's account of Christian Wise's statement to his daughter is suspiciously arch: "'It's not you, it's the money they're after, Phoebe,' he'd say over and over." Hazen tips her hand as a dramatist by claiming that Wise owned "1,000 acres of black loam, virgin timber, good buildings, and the spring." There's no evidence that Christian Wise ever owned more than 100 acres, and most of that was hillside land unsuitable for farming. A later neighbor, John Van Cura, would joke that you couldn't raise an umbrella on that land.

Young Phebe Wise, circa 1875.
Richland County Chapter of the Ohio Genealogical Society.

If Christian Wise said such things to his daughter, as the previous comments allege, it may have psychologically damaged her and led to an inability to form romantic relationships. That was certainly the assumption of many in Phebe's day, including Bromfield. A more modern perspective, though, makes one wonder about Phebe's inclinations. Could she have been a lesbian? Though she had friends of both sexes, there was never the slightest hint of any impropriety with women. Could she have been a closeted transgender person? Though she was later documented as often wearing men's clothes, those all appeared to be occasions when Phebe wore men's overalls for gardening work outside, which was simply practical. She was certainly known to parade around in fancy dresses often enough in the years to come.

One possibility that remains is that Phebe may have been what today would be described as aromantic and/or asexual. These terms are applied to people who have no interest in romantic relationships and/or sexual relationships. It is perfectly possible that Phebe fell into those categories and was quite willing to live out her life as an unmarried woman, though it can't be dismissed that she may have suffered tremendous psychological wounding in her youth at the hands of her father. The things that happened to her later, in the 1890s, would only have wounded her even further.

The 1880 census offers a few clues about the Wise family. Both Elizabeth Ann and Phebe were living with their parents at this point. Elizabeth, thirty-five, is listed by profession as a teacher. Phebe is described as being thirty-four years old, which—if correct—pushes her elusive birth date back to 1846. But unlike her sister, she is listed as working "at home." This suggests that by 1880, she had shifted from teaching to taking care of her elderly parents. It would be interesting to know which member of the household informed the census taker of this, because when asked about the birthplace of Christian Wise, the informant said he was born in Maryland, which matches other reports. But the census taker also asked for the birthplace of Christian's parents. The informant appears to have answered that they didn't have any idea where they were born, because the census taker wrote "DON'T KNOW" over those two columns for both. The break between the family and Christian's parents was significant enough that at least the Mansfield members of the family had no idea where their family originally came from.

Tragedy came to the family in July 1881, when Eliza Wise passed away from the ravages of tuberculosis. The small tower seen in the only known photograph of the Wise house—taken years later just before it was torn down in the 1930s—might have been decorative. However, it also could have been used as a general sleeping porch for any family member who found the humid summer nights unbearable. But considering Eliza's condition, it is very possible that Christian Wise built the tower as a sleeping place for Eliza, considering that the standard treatment for tuberculosis at the time was to retard the progression of the lung disease by having patients sleep

The Ohio State Reformatory, circa 1910. *Author's collection.*

exposed to cold air. The Ohio Tuberculosis Sanatorium in Mount Vernon, Ohio, was built in the early 1900s with just such a treatment plan in mind. Every dormitory had long porches where patients would be bundled up to sleep in the cold, even throughout the depths of winter. Such facilities were made obsolete by the discovery of penicillin in the mid-twentieth century. However, that was far in the future at the time of Eliza's illness, and cold air or not, she couldn't withstand the debilitating lung disease. She was buried in the family plot at Mansfield Cemetery.

Difficulties like this began to take their toll on Christian Wise, and his outlook grew darker over the years. Hazen alleges that late in life, Wise was very bitter about what he perceived as the low price he had gotten from the State of Ohio when he sold it property on which to build the Ohio State Reformatory. In fact, he had received $6,856. Adjusted for inflation, that would be the equivalent of $229,074 today. It seems that Wise's bitterness was hardly called for, but that didn't prevent him from using it to further undermine Phebe.

"Those springs are worth a million dollars," Wise is portrayed as saying. "Don't you forget that. Don't let them slickers beat you the way they did me." Whether this character in rural dialect actually had anything in common with the real Christian Wise is debatable. But we do have one source, an interview with Phebe herself, in which she confirms that her father did indeed caution her against trusting men.

So, she did not.

5

JAKE KASTANOWITZ

With her family's known prominence, Phebe Wise was bound to have men interested in becoming her suitor and, potentially, her fiancé. Her striking hauteur might have discouraged some, but there were plenty of men who took that as a challenge. Phebe, though, was not receptive. In a later interview, she gave her view on the matter: "My father always taught me to beware of all mankind," Phebe said to a *Richland Shield and Banner* reporter who encountered her on the trolley in December 1897. "Men are for the most part villains and adventurers."

She then showed a good example of her clever wit.

"You see, if I'd get married," Phebe said, "I wouldn't be Wise." The reporter said that Phebe delivered this line with "a coquettish smile and a shrug of the shoulders." Years of discourse (and, at times, sparring) with people on the streets of downtown Mansfield had given her plenty of practice in witty delivery.

Most potential suitors were turned away at the Wise house door, easily dismissed. There was one who seemed, however briefly, to have more of a chance simply because Phebe was intrigued by him. His name was Jacob Kastanowitz.

Little is known of Jake's origins, other than his birth date of September 5, 1865. Some sources claim that he was from the eastern part of the Austro-Hungarian Empire, specifically Hungary, though at least one newspaper report describes him as a "Polander." The Fairview neighborhood in which Jake and his family settled was known as "Polacktown" to locals, so the reporter may have mistakenly extrapolated from that.

What remains of the Fairview neighborhood today after several properties were flattened to make way for the Ohio Route 30 Expressway, an elevated highway crossing the Flats industrial neighborhood of Mansfield. *Author's collection.*

Jacob was born in eastern Europe on September 5, 1865, to John and Eva Kastanowitz. His parents' given names were likely Johan and Effie before they were Americanized, and his surname may have been rendered "Kastanowicz." All newspaper and city directory references to his parents give their names as John and Eva, though the death record for his mother gives her name as "Effie." His surname is frequently misspelled in newspaper reports.

Jacob's sister Mary (originally Marie) was born in January 1868. We know nothing about why the family left eastern Europe, and the only immigration record for them that has been found is one for Jacob in 1886, which confirms an origin of the Austro-Hungarian Empire for him. It's odd that only he would be listed. Perhaps he crossed separately from the others.

By 1888, the family was living in the Fairview addition, a neighborhood constructed in the late 1800s as affordable housing for immigrant factory workers. A small remnant of the neighborhood can still be found near the intersection of Longview Avenue and Wayne Street in Mansfield, but the vast majority of the development was razed in the mid-1950s during

The dead-end remnants of Jefferson Avenue. The Kastanowitz home once stood on the left, just beyond the last house. It was torn down to make way for an off-ramp from Ohio Route 30, which was later removed. *Author's collection.*

the construction of an elevated expressway that lifted U.S. 30 from the downtown streets of Mansfield to a high-speed bypass. Two-thirds of Jefferson Street were demolished for the off-ramp from U.S. 30 to OH 545. The off-ramp has since been partially removed and relocated. The lot where the Kastanowitzes lived remains buried under the remains of the off-ramp.

An 1888 city directory lists only the men of the family, as was customary at the time. Jacob is listed as a molder, referring to his job as a metal worker who molded iron stoves at the Baxter Stove Company. That company was opened in Mansfield in 1883 and brought much of its skilled workforce with it from Salem, Ohio. Jacob Kastanowitz must have made a strong impression on the Baxters, as he was hired in as a stove molder, the highest-paying job at the factory. The starting wage for a molder was $3.00 a day, which could eventually rise to $4.50, quadrupling the income of the lowest-paid employees in the factory. Such positions were highly sought after, and there must have been something about Jake, as he had become known, that led them to give him such a plum job.

We know little about Jake's youth other than the fact that multiple sources claim he was highly intelligent. One source says that Jake Kastanowitz had taught himself to read and speak seven languages, a feat that would surpass those of Phebe Wise herself. It would have been unsurprising for a young man in the Austro-Hungarian Empire to speak more than one language, as German and Hungarian were both essential, and the political importance of the empire would bring all the languages of Europe together in its borders for trade. To master seven of those languages is impressive, and it suggests that Jake had both brilliance and aspiration.

One curious thing about the 1888 city directory's listing for Kastanowitz is that his father, John, is listed, but there is only a blank space where the profession is normally listed. One wonders if he was already disabled or incapacitated, as he would later prove to be. It would have been an especially difficult relocation to the United States if the father of the family had no clear means of supporting himself, so perhaps he suffered an accident or a decline in health once the family arrived stateside. One can't help but speculate whether John was originally employed at the stove factory and suffered a crippling accident. That might explain how the young and presumably inexperienced Jake got the job.

Jake's sister Mary set herself up soon enough as a dressmaker. By the early 1890s, she was living in her own home on East Third Street and operating her dressmaking business out of her house. She must have been an enterprising entrepreneur to have her own house/business in her early twenties. Later evidence suggests that Mary was just as smart as her brother and had mastered English quickly. Her drive and aspirations would take a toll on her.

It isn't known when Jake first saw Phebe Wise, but he likely encountered her soon after settling in Fairview, as the Wise family home sat just north of Fairview, separated by only an empty field. Jake would have seen the excitement happening just north of the Wise house when construction began on the Ohio State Reformatory if he was already in Fairview by 1886. The neighborhood was bustling.

How did Jake first encounter Phebe? We do not know. In 1886, both Christian and Julia Ann were still alive, and Phebe would have had her hands full caring for them, even if she had assistance from a maid or nurse, which is possible, considering the comparative prominence of the family. But prominence does not necessarily equal wealth, and considering that many of Christian Wise's activities were in the fields of farming, preaching, and teaching, it's likely that for many years, the Wises would have had more reputation than cash in hand, though the sale of their acreage for the reformatory should have changed that. As late as 1892, a newspaper article refers to Phebe employing a maid, suggesting that their funds were still sufficient. If that is the case, the maid might have handled going into town to do the family's grocery shopping, or they may have had items delivered.

Was Phebe ever allowed to take an evening off simply for relaxation? If so, then Jake could have seen her walking along Olivesburg Road (today's Ohio State Route 545) as she headed to town. The trolley line to the reformatory was not laid until the mid-1890s, so Jake's opportunities to see Phebe may have been limited. He would likely have heard about her before he ever saw her, and gossip was rampant in Frogtown, the low-lying industrial flats on the north side of Mansfield. Just as many taverns dotted that landscape as factories, and even then, the haughty but striking Phebe Wise could have been a topic of discussion. As her parents were well-known, much speculation would have surrounded Phebe, since she was the youngest and was set to inherit the hillside property overlooking the town after her parents passed. Many men perceived her as low-hanging fruit: rich and lonely and probably looking for a man to marry her in the near future. If that's how Jake first heard of Phebe, he was in for a rude awakening.

At some point in the late 1880s, Jake became aware of Phebe and made himself known to her. This would not have been an awkward or unusual thing, considering their homes were within sight of each other, no more than a quarter of a mile apart. The Wises had long been sociable, and even after Phebe's parents were gone, she was known to entertain visitors. Jake began occasionally visiting the Wise house, most likely in the company of his mother and/or sister.

It was there that Jake first heard Phebe play the piano. It was the same square grand piano that Christian Wise had ordered to be hauled over the Appalachian Mountains from Baltimore for his children to learn to play the classics. It is reputed in folklore to have been the first piano in Mansfield, giving the small city a connection to the world of high European arts, something it has managed to maintain ever since. At the time this piano made its way to Mansfield, composers such as Frederic Chopin and Robert Schumann were still living, and Ludwig van Beethoven had only just passed away. It is perhaps this very seed that has enabled Mansfield to have an arts scene ever since. Today, that scene includes a respected regional orchestra, the Mansfield Symphony, and longstanding theater and visual arts organizations. Few towns of Mansfield's size can boast such scenes, and the Wises were a key part in establishing the arts there.

The fact that Jake showed an interest in music fired up Phebe's teaching instinct. Whenever he visited, he would ask her to play something for him. She quickly assessed his intelligence and found that while he knew little about music, his absorption of it was quick. She began to play him a different repertory to teach him about a range of classic works. Perhaps it was this special attention that prompted Jake to attempt to visit Phebe on his own. That, however, was a breach of decorum, as it would have suggested that he was formally courting her—and that was something in which she had no interest. She asked Jake to only visit with his sister.

As Jake's sister moved into her own home at some point in the late 1880s or early 1890s, she wasn't around as much for visiting, so Jake took to calling on Phebe but remained at a respectful distance away in the yard. This arrangement was initially fine for Phebe. She would simply open a window and shout out what piano piece she was playing next so that Jake could continue learning about the great composers. In time, as he began to get a grasp on the masters, he would shout back requests to Phebe. How fascinating it would be to know what pieces were played.

But Phebe's life had a major disruption on March 14, 1887. The driving force behind her extensive education and the immovable force she sometimes bristled against, her father, died. Considering that Wise's official death record only documents his age in years (instead of in the traditional format of years, months, and days), it would appear that the informant—almost certainly Phebe, as she was named the executor of his estate—did not even known his birthday.

Christian's will is an interesting document. It was written in 1864 and never updated, suggesting that his final illness caught him by surprise. He had suggested in his will that one of his sons, either George or Martin, be his executor. But in fact, they had both predeceased him by 1887. There are hints of Christian's temperament in the document. Whereas most wills of the period start off with a testament about the subject being of sound mind and then customarily moving on to some flowery blandishments about God and the soul, Christian, instead, took it as a given that he was of sound mind and starts without preamble: "My last will and testament respecting my property is as follows." Then, almost as an afterthought, he throws in the obligatory reference to commending his soul to God and then gets down to business. And his business was essentially trying to tell his heirs exactly what to do with his property not only after his death but also after his wife's death. He must have anticipated some pushback from his children, as not once but twice in the short document, he cautions them to "share and share alike" when the estate is divided after his wife's death. Probate court documents show that at the time of Christian's death, he was survived by wife, Julia A. Wise, of Mansfield; his son Frank J. Wise of Pine Bluff, Arkansas; his daughter Mary J. Ferson of Viola, Mercer County, Illinois; his daughter Ella B. Sexton also of Viola, Mercer County, Illinois; his son William H. Wise of Dunkirk, Hardin County, Ohio; and his daughter Phebe. In the text of the document, Christian lists them all by full name except for Phebe, which could be taken to suggest a contemptuous familiarity in his address of her as the family caretaker, unlike her professor and teacher siblings. On the other hand, it could also be taken as a less formal address, as she was still a teenager at the time the will was originally written.

Christian's will states that the property itself and the cash from the reformatory land sale, of which $4,630.35 remained (Wise having already advanced $500 each to his sons Franklin and William and loaned $50 each to Mary and Eliza, "for which I hold a due bill") was to be kept for future distribution. Aside from that money, he was not particularly wealthy in personal goods, as they consisted only of a handful of standard farm equipment, buggies, one cow, two stoves, all his county surveyor books and a family Bible. The probate court ruled that Julia would need some support drawn from the bank money: "And there not being sufficient property of a suitable kind to set off, we certify that the widow will need in money the sum of $300 in addition to other allowances." After funeral expenses and court costs, the total sum willed to Christian Wise's family was $3,745.44. Adjusted for inflation, that is equivalent to over $125,000 today. Christian Wise was buried in Mansfield Cemetery alongside the children who had died before him.

Phebe's mother remains an unreadable cipher to us. She outlived her husband by a little over four years without etching a distinctive profile of her own. Though stories swirl around Christian Wise and his strong personality, Julia Ann Wise slips into the background. Perhaps that was her strategy for escaping the worst of Christian's wrath. But she must have had at least some presence in the house, for even after the death of Phebe's father, Jake Kastanowitz was uneasy about visiting the Wise house when Phebe's mother was still present. In some manner, she had an imposing effect that served as a governor on Jake's infatuation. Did she perhaps remind Jake of his own mother, Eva? We'll never know.

What is known is that in the summer of 1891, Julia Ann Wise's health began to fail. The signed will in her probate court file was written with a shaky and frail hand. Phebe was to inherit the land, while the remaining money was to be split among the five living Wise children. Mary, Ella, William, Frank, and Phebe each received $550—about $18,000 today—which Phebe would have to live off for the next forty-two years. What is most interesting about this is that the full sum was $2,000 less than the amount that had been in the bank at the time of Christian's death just four years earlier. Is it perhaps from this that the legend of Phebe's profligate spending arises? If so, it shows she spent a great deal of her inheritance before she received it—and arguably spent a lot of her siblings' inheritances as well. This could very well explain their distance from her in later years, though that could also have something to do with Phebe escaping Christian's iron will and not wanting to look back. Most likely, it is a combination of the two, because if Phebe did not inherit her father's frugality, she certainly got his domineering personality. Julia Ann died of paralysis on August 26 and was buried next to Christian in the Wise family plot in Mansfield Cemetery.

Considering that the funeral expenses for Julia were nearly four times what they had been for Christian, it is likely that this was the occasion when the large obelisk was bought and engraved for the family plot. If nothing else, that gesture looks to have been a statement of love and respect from Phebe. Household items mentioned in the probate files include a glass corner cupboard, a nine-foot-long extension table, cane-seated chairs, a grandfather clock, and more. No mention is made of the piano, as it had presumably been directly gifted to Phebe long ago.

It seems that Julia Wise's death removed a governor from Jake Kastanowitz's behavior. His visits became more frequent and more insistent. Her death removed a governor from Phebe, too. With no one to stop her, she was now free to clomp up into the attic of the small house and break out her mother's carefully stored society gowns from the pre–Civil War era. Once, long ago, Julia Ann Wise had accompanied her county surveyor husband to balls, parties, and other social events, wearing the finest fashions of the day. As prominent citizens, they would have been expected to make appearances in the salons and drawing rooms of Mansfield, rubbing shoulders with politicians, bankers, industrialists, and others who populated the small but ambitious city. Julia Ann played her part exquisitely.

The young Phebe Wise had been fascinated by these fancy dresses and likely wanted more than anything to try them on herself. It appears, however, that Phebe's mother forbade her from playing with the dresses, which were only for special occasions—special occasions that no longer came once the Wise parents aged and declined in health. Julia Ann may have appreciated her daughter's abilities as a schoolteacher, but she likely saw nothing special about it. It certainly didn't merit the use of fine gowns.

For years, Phebe had longed to get her hands on those dresses and hoopskirts, to feel their folds of crinoline, taffeta, and tulle. Now, at long last, they were hers. She delightedly explored the antique garments and selected one. She tried on the dress, added as much cheap jewelry as she could carry and then strutted her way downtown.

It's possible that on one of those early excursions, Jake saw Phebe from his house, which sat on Jefferson Street, very close to the Olivesburg Road. She would have been a breathtaking vision to him, the smart and wealthy woman strolling along in impressive finery on her way to town—the woman of his dreams.

It was during this period that Phebe Wise became a familiar sight in downtown Mansfield, invariably decked out in a huge dress or sometimes layers of dresses. The old-fashioned hoopskirts were so breathtakingly fancy that some people mistook them as wedding dresses. It was also during this period that she became known for her sharp tongue. If anyone stared at her outlandish garb, she'd tear into them, often leaving behind her a trail of the sort of expletives she wasn't supposed to even know. Some were amused by the imposing nearly six-foot-tall woman. Others were made uncomfortable by her very presence, something that Phebe enjoyed.

Phebe's favorite spot to stop and observe the world was on the busy corner outside Ashbrook's Drug Store on Fourth Street. It was here that, from time to time, she would be joined by the lawyer Augustus "Gus" Douglass. While Phebe wasn't typically a big fan of lawyers, she recognized that Douglass was different. Like Phebe, Douglass didn't have much of a filter and was known to alienate people with his outspoken views. In Phebe, he found a kindred spirit, but their connection—so far as we know—was only platonic, their relationship only conducted in public, as Douglass was already married. The two enjoyed talking about politics and current events on that street corner, doubtless offering a running commentary on the fads and foibles of the passing people of Mansfield.

Douglass was ambitious enough to run for Richland County prosecutor in the mid-1890s, stepping into the formal political arena for the first time. Through no fault of his own, however, his tenure as prosecutor was doomed to be shortened by the eruption of the Ceely Rose case in Pleasant Valley, located south of Mansfield. Ceely Rose was suspected of poisoning her parents and brother, causing their deaths. When Douglass and Richland County sheriff James Boals went to Pleasant Valley to

Ashbrook's Drug Store, Phebe's favorite downtown spot to pontificate about the world with passersby. *John Sherman Room, Mansfield Richland County Public Library.*

investigate, they found themselves stymied by the unusual circumstance of a developmentally disabled young woman who was nonetheless able to avoid their efforts to prove a case against her. Given that a poisoning case presupposes a planned murder, Douglass knew that he'd have to try Ceely for murder in the first degree.

Even at that stage, before he had a confession from Ceely, Douglass probably envisioned his career in politics spinning down the toilet, as it was

North Main Street in Mansfield, the primary corridor into downtown Mansfield, Ohio. *John Sherman Room, Mansfield Richland County Public Library.*

plainly obvious to him and many others that Ceely Rose was not entirely in her right mind. Public opinion demanded a trial, justice, and punishment, while common sense made it clear that there was a slim chance of convincing a jury that Ceely approached the legal standard for sanity. Having little choice, Douglass pursued the case and finally scored a confession by coaching a friend of Ceely to spend time with her until she could get her to talk. This resulted in a confession and arrest.

When that trial began in October 1896, Gus Douglass did his best to assemble a case for murder in the first degree, producing a number of witnesses who swore that, in their opinions, Ceely Rose was of sound mind. But the defense was able to produce a score of witnesses who said they had long thought Ceely Rose was insane. The moment Douglass's political career was officially doomed was when the defense attorney, James Reed, put Douglass himself on the stand and asked him, under oath, to inform the court of how many of his prosecution witnesses who attested to Ceely's sanity were relatives of his.

They all were. Douglass lost his reelection bid and returned to loitering on the corner with Phebe Wise, becoming as bitter as she was as the years of misfortunes multiplied for the both of them. Phebe certainly recognized her kinship with this sharp-tongued lawyer, and she kept that connection open, as she would end up needing him as an advocate before the decade was out.

On the afternoon of Friday, October 16, 1891, Phebe stepped outside of her house. Like many older farmhouses, the Wise home had been built with a cellar that was only accessible from the outside. That way, vegetables could be harvested from the garden and taken directly into the root cellar for storage. They could later be fetched and taken into the house for meals. When Phebe opened the cellar door and began stepping down the stairs, she was startled at a rush of noise from within the cellar. Something was coming right at her at a high rate of speed.

Phebe's friend, attorney, and Richland County prosecutor Augustus Douglass. *John Sherman Room, Mansfield Richland County Public Library.*

It was Jake Kastanowitz. He ran at Phebe. She turned and ran back up the steps. Kastanowitz almost caught her, but she wriggled free of his grasp and took off running across the field to Ed Chatlain, her nearest neighbor. Ed had a telephone, and he let Phebe use it to call the police. Marshal O'Donnell responded and found Jake skulking about the house, so he placed him under arrest. The following day, Phebe appeared before Mansfield's mayor Newlon and gave him the long litany of escalating misbehavior from Jake since he started regularly pestering Phebe. She pointed out that even Jake's mother and sister admitted there was something mentally wrong with him. Phebe concluded by saying that she feared Jake Kastanowitz would do her bodily harm.

Jake was released that evening on his own recognizance for good behavior.

Late in 1891, Jake was brought up on mental competency charges. He was adjudged insane and sent to the Toledo State Hospital in northwest Ohio. This asylum was a modern one for its time, formed on the McBride plan, which avoided the traditional massive institutional look by spreading out the various wards into separate buildings, giving the asylum more of a neighborhood feel. Heightening the sense that the asylum was a residential area, the grounds were landscaped with beautiful plants and trees around an attractive lagoon. All of these features were designed to encourage patients' serenity and sense of normalcy, but they also attracted Toledo community members, who would often come to the asylum to picnic or boat on the lagoon.

The place certainly had a soothing effect on Jake Kastanowitz, as he quickly settled down and committed no alarming behavior. The asylum

Toledo State Hospital. *Author's collection.*

doctors quickly began to doubt that the patient should have been sent to them. Kastanowitz soon convinced the asylum doctors that he wasn't insane, and they began to discuss giving him a provisional release. Jake, however, couldn't wait for them to clear him, and he escaped from the facility on or around December 28, demonstrating the security weaknesses of the McBride system for asylums. With functions so diffused in different buildings, it was easy for Jake to walk away and his absence not be noticed until attendance was next taken.

It is not known how Jake made his way from Toledo back to Mansfield, but he did it in only one week in the middle of winter. If he walked the entire distance, he would have had to sleep either outside or in open barns, which is not impossible, though unlikely. More plausible was that he found shelter in Toledo and then hitched a ride via a buggy or train. On January 3, 1892, he was found in Mansfield, arrested by officers Patton and Moser and returned to the asylum in Toledo.

Just over a month later, Jake was declared sane by the doctors at the Toledo State Hospital and given a provisional release. By late March, Kastanowitz was again arrested and given another insanity hearing, his provisional release having already been forgotten. He was brought up in an inquest before Judge Lewis Brucker at the Richland County Courthouse. The hearing sobered Jake up briefly, and he promised the judge that he would behave. Judge Brucker discharged him, opining that his conduct was "more in the spirit of deviltry than the freaks of an insane man."

The deviltry soon escalated, however. Kastanowitz began regularly breaking into the outbuildings on the Wise farm, breaking locks in some instances. Phebe again took Jake to court on insanity charges in May 1892, alleging that he was beginning to send her offensive letters. She also said that when she rebuffed his advances, Jake would become very angry and return to her house late in the night to attempt to gain entrance. Mansfield police deputies arrested him as he left a service at the Swiss church on the corner of South Diamond and East Second Streets. Within days, Judge Brucker again released him.

On July 28, 1892, Phebe received a letter from Jake that requested her to come meet him that evening at the post office. He also included a drawing that he made with crayons, which the *Weekly News* described as "lewd in the utmost degree." The newspaper also said that the letter also contained "other obscene matter of an unmentionable character" without describing it further. It was the last of a series of letters Jake had mailed Phebe, each one bolder than the previous. Phebe took the letters to her lawyers, who opted to bypass local officials. They contacted the proper authorities in Cleveland.

By sending obscene material through the mail, Jake Kastanowitz had committed a federal offense. On August 7, 1892, deputy U.S. Marshal major A.B. Ackerman came to Mansfield with a warrant for Jake's arrest. Mansfield police marshal O'Donnell accompanied him to the Kastanowitz house on Jefferson Street early the following morning, where they arrested Jake.

At the Richland County Jail, Major Ackerman brought out the letter and drawings and asked Jake if he had sent them to Phebe Wise. Jake admitted that he wrote the letter, but despite Ackerman's repeated grilling, Jake obstinately denied drawing the lewd pictures. He claimed to know nothing about them, where they came from, or how they ended up in his letter to Phebe.

According to the *Weekly News* reporter who was present for the interrogation, Jake's only excuse for the indecency of the letter was that he expected to marry Miss Wise.

Major Ackerman took testimony from Phebe and, according to the newspaper, from a maid she employed as well. This is interesting, as it is the only indication of someone regularly working for Phebe, something not referred to elsewhere. It is unknown whether she was a part-time, full-time, or live-in maid.

On August 10, Jake was again brought up before Judge Brucker, but he waived examination, clearing the path for the federal authorities. Jake was bound over to the U.S. District Court in Cleveland. Major Ackerman escorted Kastanowitz by train to Cleveland, where he was locked up in the Cuyahoga County Jail. He was unable to furnish bail.

That stunt earned Jake a stint in the Canton Workhouse. Meanwhile, Phebe Wise was forced to deal with a much more immediate threat.

6

THE ROBBERS

At least part of what fueled Jake Kastanowitz's obsession with Phebe Wise was his impression that she was wealthy. It was a widely held assumption that she still had considerable sums of money in her possession. While she had some money, the bulk of her inheritance came in the form of property. The amount of actual money that was passed to her was modest, and Phebe's initial reaction to having no parents to squash her urge to splurge meant that she spent quite a lot of that money on clothes and things for the farm in the immediate years following their deaths.

Why this translated into a rumor that she had money hidden at her house is unclear, the only explanation being the general impression that she stood apart from the mainstream society of the town. Nonetheless, she did in fact use banks. While she kept some money on hand at her home, she hardly had piles of treasure.

That didn't keep people from thinking she did. Not only did this help fuel the dangerous obsessions of Kastanowitz, but it also incited a horrific attack that would permanently maim Phebe and intensify her sense of isolation.

A week before Christmas, on December 18, 1891, Phebe was engaged in baking some pies in her kitchen. She was hoping to finish up quickly, as dusk was falling, and in recent months, she had taken to spending her nights at neighbors' houses due to the increasing instability of Jake Kastanowitz. As he became more insistent in his attentions, Phebe began to feel vulnerable staying at home alone. Fortunately, her neighbors welcomed her on the nights she didn't want to be alone. That evening, she aimed to finish up her baking and head out before full darkness fell.

When she heard an odd noise around the front door, she likely assumed it was another visit from Jake and that she'd be able to get him to relent by yelling at him. As she made her way from the kitchen into the sitting room, the door suddenly splintered open, and Phebe saw that it wasn't Jake at all. Three men, all wearing cloth masks, forced their way into the little house. The three surrounded her, grabbed her and pointed revolvers at her head, saying that if she uttered a sound, she would be shot.

The men demanded her money. Phebe replied that she would go into the other room to fetch it for them. Her plan, however, was to step into the room where she knew she had a revolver. The robbers sussed out the nature of her plan and decided to search the place themselves.

A dramatization of robbers entering Phebe's house from *Phoebe* (the robbers were played by Jeff Dowdy and Chris Mollica). *Author's collection.*

They took the sheet from her bed and tore it into strips, which they used to tie her arms and legs together. They used a rope they had brought in with them to tie Phebe's hands together. They used a piece of sheet to gag the woman and undertook a chaotic search, opening drawers and slashing cushions. For over an hour, they tore apart the house in search of money. They found nothing. One of the offenders removed the gag and asked her where she kept her cash. Phebe refused to answer, even after one of the robbers, whom Phebe later described as "the one with a black beard," grabbed her by the throat.

After several unsuccessful tries, the head robber took the crime to a cruel new level. He had the others grab Phebe's legs and raise her feet. He took a candle from the table, where it sat in a brass candlestick, and threatened to burn the woman's feet if she didn't tell them where the money was. She said nothing. The robber moved the taper to Phebe's feet and placed the flame against her skin, slowly moving it around. She remained stoic as long as she could, the torture progressing from severe burning to actual smoking as the flame charred her skin.

At this point, the robbers threatened to pick her up and sit her down on the red-hot stove where her pies had just recently finished baking. She finally gave in and told them where her only valuable jewelry—a gold watch and chain that had belonged to her father—and a small stash of cash were. When the first reports of the robbery came out, the watch was described as being valued at $100 and the cash amounting to only $10. Later reports cite that the total value of the items stolen was over $500, so it isn't clear whether this early report was incorrect due to mistaken information or outright misinformation from either Phebe herself or the police. While it might not exactly amount to the legend of treasure, a haul of $110 in 1891 would be the equivalent of over $3,600 today, over 130 years later. A $500 sum would be valued over $15,000 today.

After a further search of the house, the three offenders discussed killing Phebe. One of the three was in favor of the idea of shooting her; while another, whom Phebe perceived as the youngest, was upset by the idea and begged his cohorts not to do it. They relented and said that if she tried to leave after they left, they'd shoot her.

Before leaving, they decided to pause and eat one of the pies that Phebe had been baking. Curiously, the young robber turned and politely asked Phebe if they could have some pie before they left. Phebe nodded, and the criminals helped themselves. Upon leaving, they told her they would stay by her house and shoot her if she dared step out. They left her tied up.

After untying herself, Phebe waited a long time before venturing outside. There was no sign of the robbers. Barely able to walk, she made her way toward Fairview and the Erie Railroad telegraph office. There, she wired the police around 9:00 p.m. and told them of the crime. Marshal O'Donnell and Officers Dise and Culbertson responded to the scene.

In their investigation, the police found the metal jimmy that had been used to force the front door open lying on a table in the house. A well-worn workman's glove was found the following day in the second round of searching.

The robbers didn't exactly make it difficult for the police to track them down, as the first thing they did was go down the hill into the Flats to hit the saloons. There, they flashed around and spent a great deal of cash. As the police began investigating, they were told that four men, Henry Zweifel, "Zip" Tyler, Ike Hartman, and Tom Bloor, were using an empty barn on the north side of Mansfield as a hangout and rendezvous point.

The police raided the barn the following Saturday, but the four men ran in separate directions. Zweifel hopped on a westbound Pennsylvania Railroad train, escaping the officers. The police wired ahead to have him sent back to Mansfield on the next train. Upon Zweifel's return the following day, the police interrogated him. Getting no admissions from him and having no solid proof, the police were forced to release him. Zweifel immediately shaved his beard, leaving his long mustache, and left town on a train headed north before sunset that Sunday.

Another of the group, a "notorious character" named William "Zip" Tyler, was picked up by police in the Flats and arrested that Monday afternoon. Later that evening, a Super's Livery Stable employee, Ike Hartman, and a young man named Tom Bloor, "who has been hanging around town for several days," were arrested. When a man by the name of Ed Wolfarth attempted to bring the arrested men tobacco and pipes, he was arrested, too. The men were overheard arguing in the county jail, accusing each other of giving up information.

Bloor was known to have had a considerable sum of cash on Saturday, but he had largely spent it by Monday evening. When questioned, he claimed it was money he had received as a loan, though he could produce nothing to prove this.

Wolfarth was released that Tuesday morning, and Hartman was released not long after that, as it was believed that while the two men appeared to know something about the crime, neither appeared to be one of the direct offenders. It was soon revealed why the police released Wolfarth and Hartman: under questioning, Tom Bloor confessed to being one of the three robbers. He said that he, Zip Tyler, and Henry Zweifel were the robbers who broke into Phebe Wise's house, tortured her, and stole her money and jewelry. Bloor said they had left the Flats around 5:00 p.m. with the intention of going up the hill to Phebe's house to steal her treasure. He accurately described the jimmy they used to open the door and the interior of Phebe's house.

Tyler refused to answer questions from the police and pleaded not guilty when the two were arraigned that Tuesday evening. Bloor initially pleaded guilty, though he later changed his plea to not guilty.

That same evening, Marshal O'Donnell questioned Zweifel's acquaintances in the Flats about his possible whereabouts. Informants told him to search for a man using the name "C.C. Skyles," which was the name Zweifel used to join the cigar makers' union in South Bend, Indiana, in 1885. This clue turned out to be the key, as O'Donnell found that "Skyles" had used his union identification card to borrow $2.25 for travel expenses, charged against union card number 38722. He had departed Mansfield for Port Huron, Michigan.

From Port Huron, the trail led to Monroe, Michigan, where O'Donnell found numerous people who placed Zweifel there not long before

O'Donnell arrived that Thursday evening. With the help of the local police chief, O'Donnell discovered that C.C. Skyles had just started working for Chambers and Mudford, cigar makers, and was due to arrive at work the following morning at nine o'clock.

The following morning, Zweifel, alias Skyles, arrived at work and began rolling cigars. He was only about a dozen cigars into his morning work when he was pointed out to Marshal O'Donnell. The Mansfield policeman quietly walked up to him and stood next to him, saying nothing. Zweifel kept working, refusing to acknowledge the presence of the policeman next to him. O'Donnell finally spoke to him and informed him that he was wanted for questioning regarding a crime that had taken place in Mansfield, Ohio. Zweifel said nothing. O'Donnell had a local policeman arrest Zweifel.

When they got Zweifel to the station, they found that he had five dollars in cash on him and that his union credit book had been maxed out at twenty dollars. When the police told Zweifel what crime he was being detained for, he denied even knowing where Phebe Wise lived, let alone breaking into her house. Seemingly not worried about the accusation, he simply said that he was not guilty of the crime. While this questioning was going on, other officers were checking into his name. It turns out that Zweifel had previously served a term in the Michigan State Prison at Jackson for burglary. As recently as two months prior, he had been fined for drunkenness in Cincinnati.

He said he wanted to get the matter cleared up as quickly as possible, so he went willingly with O'Donnell, not requiring full legal extradition. O'Donnell said that the prisoner was no trouble during the return train trip. In Mansfield, he was bound over to common pleas court with a bond of $2,500, which he could not pay. He then went to the Richland County Jail to await final arraignment and trial.

On April 14, 1892, as law enforcement officials were taking Zweifel and Tyler to be arraigned, they left one of the two doors leading from the cells unlocked. This in itself would not have been important, except that the sheriff's wife came in to clean the cell and left the outer door unlocked. Thus, while Mrs. Tressel was occupied, Tom Bloor was able to quietly step out of his cell and make his way downstairs in the Richland County Jail. Since he acted confidently, like he was on an assigned errand, no one noticed him. He walked through the jail kitchen, grabbing a couple of handfuls to eat as he did so, and walked out the back door of the jail.

A couple of workers who were excavating a site behind the jail in preparation for the construction of a new barn recognized Bloor. The men

Richland County Jail. *Author's collection.*

alerted the police, who immediately sent out Marshal O'Donnell and Officer Friesh in a buggy to chase Bloor. They quickly found him. Bloor attempted to leave the roadway and cut across fields, but the policemen were able to catch up with him and return him to jail, where he was arraigned for the additional charge of jailbreak.

One might think that this escape would have led to tighter controls in the Richland County Jail, but they would be wrong. On April 28, Zip Tyler walked out of the place and was never seen again. This—and subsequent escapes—doomed the career of Sheriff Tressel, who lost his reelection bid to James Boals.

Bloor went on trial before Judge Norman Wolfe on the charge of burglary. His lawyer, J.P. Seward, pleaded for the court's mercy, stating that the defendant had been the tool of a hardened criminal, presumably referring to Zweifel. Seward further said that mercy was called for, considering that Bloor had been cooperative, giving the police the key information needed to break the case. The judge agreed and sentenced Bloor to the minimum term of one year of hard labor.

He was then tried on the burglary charge. Phebe Wise was called to the stand, where she said that she recognized the voice of the leader of the trio of bandits, Zweifel, because he had come to her house about a month before the incident and asked her some random questions about various local people, as if he were a traveler looking for someone. Phebe's neighbor Joe Patton testified that he saw Zweifel talking to Phebe Wise that day and also noticed another man in the woods nearby, whom he recognized as Tom Bloor. Their visit had apparently been a reconnaissance of the Wise property. On the stand, Bloor said that they had been planning the crime for weeks. When they came up to Phebe's house on December 18, they did not expect her to be there, as they had observed that she normally stayed with neighbors at night. When they jimmied open the door, they were very surprised to see her there and improvised from there on out, following Zweifel's lead. Once Phebe finally confessed to them that the money was hidden behind a loose board on the stairwell, Zweifel pried the board open and found $350.

According to Bloor, Zweifel pocketed the money, the watch, the gold chain, and a diamond ring that they found while ransacking the place. Bloor met up with him that Saturday morning and was given his share of eighty-five dollars, Zweifel announcing that he was going to keep "the lion's share." By his own description, Bloor took his money and began "blowing it," running through thirty-five dollars in one day. He then gave the remaining fifty dollars to a bartender to keep for him. When Tyler was arrested, he had no money on him.

Reading the writing on the wall from the trial of his cohort, Zweifel pleaded guilty to all charges when he finally came up for trial in May. Prosecutor Gus Douglass said that some mercy could be allowed due to his guilty plea, though it remained evident that Zweifel was a career criminal.

Judge Wolfe lectured the man.

Ten years ago, you stood here in this very courthouse charged with the crime of larceny, and if you had not committed burglary, it was a mere technicality which saved you. Again a few years ago, you stood before the court in another county charged with a serious crime. Ten years ago, in passing sentence upon you, the court here said it was intended to reform you, and the court of Wayne County said the same thing. If you could be corrected by a light sentence, it would be much better for you, for good citizens are what Mansfield wants. You have put yourself beyond the pale of mercy in this crime. You inflicted punishment for your own gain of a few dollars that would have challenged the admiration of a barbarian. You must have studied the custom of barbarians to inflict such torture upon that lone woman. I believe you to be the leader of the men who committed the crime, one of whom is now in the penitentiary, and one who should be who is at large. If you have the slightest chance to speak a word to young Bloor, you ought to tell him to do better. I am asked to have mercy for one who has no mercy in his heart—Henry Zweifel, but I believe your pleading guilty should shorten your sentence at least two years. You will therefore be committed to the state penitentiary for eight years, no part of it at solitary confinement but all of it at hard labor.

When Zweifel arrived at the Ohio Penitentiary in Columbus, Deputy Warden Playford was furious to find that the prisoner was so drunk, he could barely stand up. Richland County deputy sheriff Guthrie admitted that he had given the prisoner some whiskey to help him "brace up" but denied that the prisoner was truly drunk. A Columbus newspaper disagreed, stating that Zweifel's breath was just about strong enough "to knock a guard off the wall." Zweifel served his time working in the prison's cigar making shop.

Henry Zweifel was born in Oshkosh, Wisconsin, in 1857, the son of Swiss immigrants Fridelin and Regula Zweifel, whose first names had been Americanized to Fred and Rachel. After his parents died, along with a number of his siblings, Zweifel seems to have become destabilized, becoming involved in a number of crimes throughout the Midwest. As early as 1880, he was arrested in Bucyrus in Crawford County for a crime committed in Mansfield. When the police arrived to take him to Mansfield, they searched him and found a concealed altered key, which he presumably meant to use to escape. In 1881, he was noted as having broken out of the Richland County Jail while he was incarcerated for another crime. Perhaps it was for that crime that he served a term of three years in the Ohio Penitentiary for burglary. He additionally spent some time in the Ashland County Jail for a burglary committed in Loudonville, but he broke out of there with a group of escaping inmates. After declaring that he wanted to "live square," he got a job at one of Mansfield's cigar making factories, and remarkably, the escape charges were dropped. Unfortunately, shortly after that, he was put on trial for manslaughter in Canton due to an incident that occurred in Massillon, but he was acquitted on that charge. About a year after that came the Phebe Wise torture and robbery case.

After Zweifel completed his sentence in Ohio for Phebe's case, there's no indication that he turned over a new leaf—or even tried to do so. In 1897, Zweifel was again arrested in Mansfield on a charge of disturbing the peace. In 1899, he was arrested again for burglary in Mansfield, this time under his old alias Skyles. He was also recorded as occasionally using the fake name "C. Brown." After this, he was falsely accused of being one of the offenders in a robbery that took place in Gallipolis in 1902, but Zweifel denied all involvement. He explained his continuing visits to Mansfield as trips to see his brother John, who lived there. John also had run-ins with the law and was sent to the Ohio Penitentiary in 1907 for shooting at a Mansfield police officer with intent to kill.

Thomas H. Bloor was a lifelong Mansfield resident. He was born in 1871 to Thomas and Mahala Bloor, but his father died while Tom was still an infant. Subsequent records show that Bloor was again arrested on burglary charges in 1895. Later census reports show that he lived with his mother until she died in 1920. They also show that he had a spotty employment record as a carpenter and, at times, bartender, suggesting he never cut his longstanding ties with the Flats. In his later years, he, at times, rented rooms to other men, and he never married. He died around the age of sixty in 1932.

William Tyler, who was known to be three or more years older than Bloor, remains otherwise obscure. He was noted in the local news a few times before his crime against Phebe. As early as 1885, he was sentenced to the Cleveland Workhouse for petit larceny. In 1889, he made headlines for his unusual living quarters

> *"Zip" Tyler, a well-known character around town, has been without a home for some time and has built a cave in the woods on Park Avenue East. He has furnished his residence in real Robinson Crusoe style and eats and sleeps in one apartment. A number of the residents in the east end of the city called on "Zip" yesterday and were well entertained. "Zip" has been a child of misfortune. In his early days he had the opportunity of an education, but did not embrace it. Having no person he could call father, his mother was not very strict with him, and he soon fell into bad ways. He is now about twenty-five years old and seems to enjoy his hermitage.*

In 1890, Zip was thrown out of an opera house in Mansfield for causing a disturbance. After leaving, he proceeded to a hardware store with the stated intention of buying a knife and returning to the opera house to stab the usher who threw him out. The police were alerted, and a patrolman attempted to arrest Tyler, who fought back wildly. After finally wiggling out of his coat, Tyler took off running, leaving the policeman holding his jacket. Then, a year later, after his jailbreak, Tyler was never seen again in Mansfield. One can only presume that he moved elsewhere and started a new life under a new name.

Phebe Wise was disturbed that one of the gang members was still at large and worried for some time that he might return to the area to take his revenge on her. However, she soon found her hands full with Jake Kastanowitz and no longer had the time to worry about Tyler. Jake was becoming an equal if not a greater threat.

Nonetheless, the physical effect of the crime remained. Neighbor John Van Cura later told genealogist Marji Hazen that Phebe never entirely recovered from the robbery.

"Phoebe was so bent over that you couldn't any more straighten her back up than a warped shingle on a house," Van Cura said. "That was bent and was going to stay that way forever. After they tortured her, she was always crippled and could never straighten up after that. She was always careful of how she walked and what she did. The abuse was what brought her down to where she was. After a person goes through an ordeal like that, they can't forget."

7

THIS IS GOING TO END
ONE OF TWO WAYS

T he rest of 1892 and the beginning of 1893 saw Jake's continued
pressing of his case with Phebe Wise—with subsequent ineffective
punishments.

In early 1893, the health of Jake's sister Mary took a turn for the worse,
and she had a last will and testament drawn up, even though she was only
twenty-four. Presumably, a lawyer provided some of the legalese of the
document, but there is a note along the bottom where a witness recorded
that upon reading the document, Mary crossed out one word, correcting
the grammar of the document and suggesting that she was very fluent in the
English language, despite the family's late immigration. There are a couple
of intriguing points in the document. When Mary talks about splitting up
her estate, she names her parents as the ones to inherit her house on East
Third Street in Mansfield (interestingly, just a few blocks down the road
from young Lewis Brumfield, who would soon figure prominently in Phebe
Wise's story). This suggests she was very well aware that her illness was very
likely to end her life before her parents died. She also left a partial interest to
her brother Jacob "if he is still living." There would seem no reason for her
to add such a phrase unless she thought it might be possible that no matter
how ill she was, there was a chance her brother could die first. It is a strong
indication that all the family members were all too painfully aware of Jacob's
precipitous decline into madness.

A photograph of Phebe discouraging Jake from the historical drama *Phoebe* (Jake was played by Thaynne Olsen; Phebe Wise was played by Chevy Troxell Bond). *Author's collection.*

Mary died on March 30, 1893, from heart failure. It's no surprise that in the wake of this loss, Jake's behavior grew even more erratic. In July 1893, Phebe once again petitioned the court to hold an inquest regarding Jake's mental condition, though they didn't arrest Jake until late August. On September 9, Jake Kastanowitz was once again deemed insane and sent once more to the Toledo State Hospital. After a few months, he was back home, and he made a beeline for Phebe's house.

The authorities decided to take a different tack when he was brought up on charges in August 1894. Phebe said in court that if Kastanowitz was not found insane and sent away, she was going to press charges against him for physical assault. Noting that Jake's previous trips to Toledo had proven ineffective, the officials concluded that his behavior was due less to insanity and more to sheer cussedness. This time, Judge Brucker sentenced Jake to a term in the Canton Workhouse in Stark County.

That held Jake for over a year, but when he returned to Mansfield, it wasn't long before he was in trouble again. On this occasion, though, he was charged by someone other than Phebe Wise. One day in March 1896,

Richland County Courthouse. *Author's collection.*

two thirteen-year-old girls who lived in Fairview, Jennie Shuster and Helen Poleski, went to the Kastanowitz house to have milk. While they were there, Jacob made a comment about Jennie's older sister and used "very indecent language." The girl testified that Kastanowitz also repeatedly instructed her to call Phebe Wise bad names. The other girl did not show up for the hearing.

Jake was called to the stand, where he denied it all and said that he was not guilty.

Defense counsel John W. Leidigh then attempted to put Jake's mother, Eva, on the stand. Eva refused to take an oath on religious grounds and grew very upset about the request. Thinking the difficulty was due to Eva's limited understanding of English, a translator was brought in. For half an hour, the translator, John Bartenfels, attempted to get Eva to affirm the testimony she was about to give. Eva got in a high dudgeon about this, stating that an affirmation was the same thing as an oath, no matter how much Bartenfels insisted it was the only way for the trial to go forward. After a strenuous effort, they were able to get Eva to leave religion out of it and simply state that she would be telling the truth in her testimony.

Once that was settled, it was discovered that the entire conversation between Jake and the girls had been held in English, which Eva did not understand. Jake's father, John, was put on the stand—with the same result.

"The court and everybody in it were tired by this time," a reporter for the *Semi Weekly News* wrote, "and the mayor issued a summons for Helen Poleski and continued the case until she can be brought into court." After the case was resumed, Jake was found guilty and fined five dollars, plus court costs.

In August, Jake was given a three-month jail sentence for breaking into Phebe's home. He was quietly released in early November. No one was informed of his release; thus, Phebe suffered a terrible surprise when he suddenly showed up at her house on the evening of Sunday, November 7. Though the weather was cold and windy, he maintained his vigil, repeatedly asking Phebe to let him in, no matter how many times he rebuffed him. The *Richland Shield and Banner* savored the strange news, writing, "It was a frosty wind and Jacob became quite cold, although his ardor was sizzling hot."

Unable to stand the cold any longer, Jake attempted to break into the house through the front door. Having already threatened to shoot Jake, Phebe had her Winchester rifle ready. As he was pounding on the door, she pulled the trigger. The gun misfired. Five more times, she tried the trigger, and the rifle failed to go off. Hearing the clicks of the rifle finally prompted Jake to give up for the evening, and he made a hasty retreat. As the *Semi Weekly News* put it, "The only reason that Jacob is not wearing a wooden overcoat

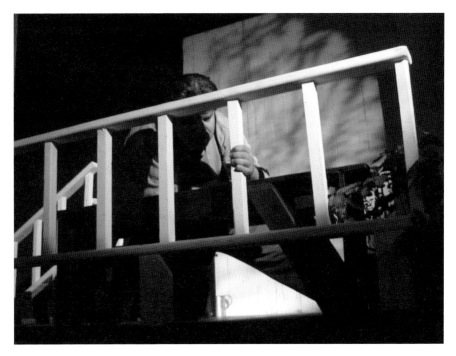

A dramatization of Jake's unraveling on Phebe's porch from *Phoebe* (Jake was played by Thaynne Olsen). *Author's collection.*

decorated with chrysanthemums is because the Winchester repeating rifle failed to explode."

Jake fleeing wasn't quite enough for Phebe. Though she was still partially lame from her wounds sustained in the robbery and was also suffering rheumatism as she aged, Phebe flung open the door and chased Jake down the road to Fairview. She relented only after he retreated into his house on Jefferson Street.

Disappointed, Phebe went back home. On another occasion soon thereafter, the Winchester worked when she shot at Jake; the bullet clipped him, leaving a superficial wound on his arm that caused him to scream but barely dampened his enthusiasm for nightly visits.

On Thursday, August 26, 1897, Phebe registered yet another complaint about receiving obscene letters from Jake. She said that he threatened "all manner of terrible things" if his love was spurned. A later article confirmed that these included death threats. Marshal Patton made a trip out to the reformatory before Phebe returned home and corralled Jake, who smiled as he was being arrested.

Just before Christmas 1897, a newspaper reporter encountered Phebe on the Diamond Street trolley as it headed out toward the reformatory. After some cheerful banter between the two, Phebe brought up the stressful situation with Jake Kastanowitz, which was widely known throughout the town.

"I never passed such a night in all my life as I did Sunday night," she said to the reporter.

"What was the trouble?" he said.

"Trouble enough, I dare say. That Jake was around my house all night, trying to break in the front door. I didn't sleep a wink all night. Oh, no! I wasn't scared, because I had my Winchester ready, and I had a good notion to shoot him if it hadn't been that Mayor Henry told me the day before that he would send someone after Jake, I believe I would have shot him."

The reporter repeated the generally held opinion of the situation.

"From the way he pesters you, Miss Wise, there are only two remedies that can be suggested."

"What are they?" Phebe asked eagerly.

"You will either have to marry him or kill him!"

"Well, I'll never marry him," she said.

At that point, she broke off and shouted at the trolley motorman, who had just passed her house. The motorman apologized profusely and made sure to drop her off on the return from the nearby reformatory.

On the afternoon of Sunday, May 22, 1898, Phebe was entertaining a few visiting women when Jake Kastanowitz showed up in her yard. He sang and shouted for a bit but then seemed to grasp that Phebe had visitors and grew quiet. When the visitors made for the front door to leave, Jake attempted to conceal himself in the hedge that ran along the edge of the yard. He singularly failed at making himself inconspicuous, as the visitors could plainly see him and called out their goodbyes to him as they left.

Once the visitors had walked a good distance down the road, Jake climbed out of the hedge and began singing loudly and calling Phebe his "baby." As evening gathered, he moved closer to the house and attempted to look in the windows with his wire technique that he used to move the curtains. Phebe told him to leave, or she would shoot him with her rifle. He left.

The remainder of the evening was quiet, and Phebe went upstairs to go to bed. Around midnight, she heard a sound that she recognized as someone fiddling with a window downstairs. Alarmed that Jake or some other intruder might break in, she got out of bed, picked up her .32-caliber Winchester rifle and cautiously made her way down the stairs and into the parlor. At the foot of the stairs, she could tell that the sounds were coming from the kitchen on the north side of the house.

She slowly advanced into the kitchen, holding the gun in front of her. As soon as she stepped into the room, a voice just outside the kitchen window burst into an off-kilter song. It was Jake. He was somehow standing at the window, even though the foundation of the house placed the kitchen window high off the ground. He had pushed the curtain aside with a wire run through one of three holes he had drilled through the sash. Phebe yelled at him to stop, leave her alone, and go home. Jake said he would not stop until she married him.

"You've got as much right to marry me tonight as any time," Jake shouted through the window. "You'll either marry me or kill me."

Phebe brandished the gun and warned him that if he did not stop, she would shoot him.

For a brief moment that must have felt like an eternity, they stared at each other through the kitchen window. Then Jake suddenly roared and grabbed the window frame, shaking it with such violence that Phebe thought he might rip the entire window out of the wall.

In an automatic reaction to Jake's rage, Phebe pulled the trigger. The rifle fired, deafeningly loud. Jake yelled as he twisted away from the window. She heard the thud of his body hitting the ground.

Then there was silence.

Jake was no longer standing at the window. There was a bullet hole through the frame of the window, where the upper and lower panes met. Two panes of glass were shattered. She thought she heard a faint groan. She didn't dare go to see what had happened, because she suspected that it might be a trap. If she stepped outside the house, she would be vulnerable to him jumping on her from the side. Even if she went over to the window and looked out, he might come hurtling through the window, which was now broken. After all, he had somehow gotten himself up to the mid-level window, perhaps using a small ladder. She stood there for what seemed an eternity until she couldn't hold the gun anymore. Not hearing or seeing anything else, she finally made her way back upstairs and crawled into bed.

She could not sleep. She thought she heard a distant, faint moan. She kept hearing it periodically throughout the interminable night, but she couldn't take the risk of going outside to investigate. She continued listening as the hours crawled past, not sleeping. The noise stopped just before dawn.

Around 9:00 a.m., a buggy rode up. Elmer Terman was in the buggy, and he was making the rounds, looking at properties to make tax assessment lists for Madison Township. Terman approached the front door of the Wise house and knocked. He got no answer, and the house was utterly still. He knocked again—nothing. He looked at the windows and noticed a few holes drilled in them, doubtless the work of Phebe's tormentor, Jake Kastanowitz, whom everyone in town knew about, thanks to newspaper coverage.

Although he figured there was a chance Phebe might be out tending to chores in the barn, Terman didn't want to leave without making sure everything was okay, considering the signs of Jake's recent presence. The young man's increasing instability was a subject of much talk in the town. Terman figured the best thing he could do was go around to the side of the house, in case Phebe was working in the kitchen and couldn't hear him knocking. The kitchen, on the north side of the house, had a door on which he could knock.

He rounded the corner and froze. For a second, the scene must have been inexplicable. There were two piles of bricks on the ground, with a wide plank stretched across the top of the piles. The entire improvised structure sat beneath the shattered kitchen window. It was a platform that one could stand on to look inside the window, which otherwise would have been too far off the ground to look into. The bottom sash of the window had three small holes drilled in it. A stiff wire was protruding from one of the holes.

Just in front of the structure, sprawled out on his stomach in a large pool of blood where he had fallen from his platform perch, was Jacob Kastanowitz. He was dead.

After recovering from a moment of shock, Terman rushed around the corner and bellowed for help. Farmer W.W. Stewart was nearby, and he rushed over to see what Terman was upset about. Stewart was equally aghast at the scene. Both men knew Kastanowitz from the neighborhood and from Phebe's plight. They quickly examined him, confirming that he was indeed dead. He had a bullet wound in his shoulder with no evident exit wound. He had bled out on the ground. His body was stiff with rigor mortis.

They quickly left the body and started knocking on every door and window, calling for Phebe. They were afraid that after shooting Jake, she might have become consumed with guilt and died by suicide, or perhaps he had wounded her in an altercation before she shot him. Getting no answer, the men decided to drive into town to alert the police and the Richland County coroner, George Baughman.

The coroner gathered a team to investigate, including Constable Winters and Officers O'Donnell and Madden. A *Richland Shield and Banner* reporter was evidently at the police department when news of the killing came in, as he accompanied the officials out to the Wise farm on the streetcar. The motorman dropped them off at the bottom of the hill by the spring, and they made their way up the hillside, through the outbuildings, and to the house. They found Jake's body just outside the kitchen window.

Coroner Baughman turned Kastanowitz's body over and carried out a preliminary examination, confirming that he was dead.

"She did a good job," Baughman said, examining Kastanowitz's wound. He opined that Jake was dead before he hit the ground. Searching the man's pockets, he found only a coin purse, a small lead pencil, and a streetcar transfer.

They went around to the front of the house, knocking on the door and ringing the doorbell. Receiving no answer, they, too, tried other doors and windows but found them locked. The coroner ordered the door to be broken into. Officer O'Donnell used his shoulder to break the door wide open.

Officer Madden made a search of the upstairs area. He unwrapped an oddly shaped comforter bundle and found Phebe's Winchester rifle, containing one spent cartridge and several fresh ones. Down in the kitchen, Officer O'Donnell found a rusty revolver hidden under a cabinet, along with a box of .32-caliber rifle cartridges.

At that point, Richland County sheriff James Boals and County Prosecutor W.H. Bowers arrived on the scene. Boals said that he had heard a rumor that Phebe had left the house and gone into town early that morning. They left one of the officers on duty as a guard and headed down the street to the nearest undertaker.

Coroner Baughman had Kastanowitz's body removed to Charles Schroer and Sons for the postmortem examination. The exam was conducted by Drs. Mecklem and Schambs. They found that the bullet entered Jake's right shoulder, breaking his collar bone, and then taken a downward path into his lungs. Part of this trajectory was caused by Jake's bent posture at the window and part of it was caused by the bullet's deflection off his collar bone. In his first statement to the press, Coroner Baughman said that the bullet had severed Jake's subclavian artery and vein and that if he didn't die instantly, he could not have lasted longer than five minutes.

Richland County sheriff James Boals. *John Sherman Room, Mansfield Richland County Public Library.*

Prosecutor Bower and the newspaper reporter went to the Kastanowitz home on Jefferson Street. Eva Kastanowitz answered the door, but the two men were unable to communicate with her. The woman spoke no English, but she took them two doors down the street to the Zedigers' house, where Mrs. Zediger was able to translate. The prosecutor asked her if she knew the present whereabouts of her son, Jacob. She said she did not. He asked when she had last seen him, and she replied that he had left the house around five o'clock the previous evening, just after dinner, but had not returned all night.

At this point, Eva realized something was seriously wrong. She demanded Mrs. Zediger ask the official what was going on with her son. Prosecutor Bower informed her that Phebe Wise had shot him and that he was dead.

Eva cried and bemoaned the loss of her only son, the only child she'd had left. She railed against Phebe Wise.

"Well, she lured him on and killed him," Eva said through the translator. "She should bury him."

By this point, Jake's father, John, had joined them. The man was feeble and in poor health. Eva said they had no money, as John was unable to do much work. She said that Jake had his own room in their house on Jefferson Street and that he never kept late hours. She knew something was wrong when he didn't come home the previous evening after stepping out around 5:00 p.m. He was normally in bed by 9:00 p.m., and when she discovered that morning that he had never come home, she knew something was wrong. She had been considering heading into town to alert the police of her son's disappearance when Bowers knocked on her door.

She said her son had turned thirty-two the previous September 5 and that he had been in the United States for seventeen years, which meant he had immigrated in 1881. She confirmed that the family was from Austro-Hungary.

Eva said that her son often told her that he didn't care for Phebe Wise; he only went there to hear her play the piano, which she did beautifully. She said he told her Phebe would let him into the house and play for him. She claimed that's the only reason he went to her house.

As John and Eva continued to speak with the prosecutor and the reporter, they conveyed that they had been afraid something like this would happen. They didn't express any more blame against Phebe Wise and said that they had simply prepared for the worst. The reporter noted that they were the poorest family on Jefferson Street.

The *Shield* reporter made an oblique comment at the end of his article that seems significant: "There is little doubt that the man was crazy, as the evidences of physical infirmities [marking] his body were many and showed that he practiced those habits which tend towards softness of the brain," the reporter wrote. "The man was really a revolting sight as Coroner Baughman's party viewed him Monday morning, but a description of it could not be couched in language suitable for a refined reader. It was truly the case of a man's lust dragging him down, unfitting him for decent life, and finally resulting in his awful death."

The language around "habits tending toward softness of the brain" sound like a euphemism for masturbation, though it isn't clear how such a habit would be evident during a cursory examination of a body. It's more likely Kastanowitz showed signs of cutting and self-mutilation, perhaps extending to his own genitals. It's hard to imagine how this comment could have been provoked otherwise.

Meanwhile, other officers had begun a sweep through downtown, looking for any sign of Phebe. After the police were seen on South Main Street, Mrs. Hoover turned from the window of her house to the friend she had been calming down and comforting over coffee since just after six o'clock that morning: Phebe Wise. She gently told Phebe that she needed to let the police know that she was OK in order to begin sorting out the terrible events. Martin Hoover volunteered to accompany her to the nearest police station. They flagged down Marshal Patton and Patrolman John Huber.

It turns out that as soon as dawn had broken, Phebe had gotten dressed and left her house, crossing behind the south side of the house to walk down to the streetcar tracks. She completely avoided checking to see what had happened to Jake Kastanowitz. She marched down the hill and flagged down the first streetcar of the day, which had made its early run to the reformatory, departing there at 6:02 a.m.

The motorman was surprised to see Phebe out and about.

"You're out early today," he said.

"Yes," Phebe answered tersely before sitting down. She said not one word more for the entire ride into town. She got off the streetcar on South Main Street and made her way to the Hoovers, where she told them what happened before going with the police.

At the police station, Phebe explained that she had shot Kastanowitz, and then the officers accompanied her to Mayor Henry's court, where she told the story again at 1:30 p.m. One of the officers in court pointed out that he had seen Phebe at church the day before and that she had complained to him about Jake's continued harassment. The policeman said that he advised Phebe at that time to do whatever she had to do to protect herself. The mayor said that, of course, there would have to be a formal inquest but

The streetcar that ran from downtown Mansfield to the reformatory. Phebe often flagged down the trolley and rode for free. *John Sherman Room, Mansfield Richland County Public Library.*

that he'd be very surprised if any charges were levied against her. She was released on her own recognizance.

Mansfielder George Rowe later said that his father, who worked at the Ohio State Reformatory, heard the fatal shot that killed Jake Kastanowitz that night. Since the sound of the shot came from a distance, off the reformatory's grounds, he made no further investigation. A resident of Fairview claimed to have heard a gunshot around 7:00 p.m. but was not backed up by anyone else.

The day after the incident was discovered, a formal arraignment was held at the mayor's court. Over three hundred spectators crowded into the small courtroom, and the *Shield* reporter said that the crowd was plainly there to support Phebe, who showed up early. She seemed nervous but in good spirits. Former prosecutor Gus Douglass and other lawyers were on hand to support Phebe. The state's prosecutor was H.W. Bowers.

The mayor got things underway by swearing Phebe in and asking her about her representation.

"Have you an attorney?" Mayor Henry said.

"No sir," Phebe said. "I need none."

"If you want one, Miss Wise, I will see that one is provided for you."

"No, thank you," she said. "I don't care for any."

He then asked the next routine question: "How old are you?"

"I have never seen a record of my age," she replied. The crowd snickered as the mayor smiled.

"Probably forty or thirty-five," Henry said generously. Phebe was likely around fifty at this time.

"I am more than sixteen," Phebe said, "I know that."

"Well, I'll mark it sixteen-plus," Henry said.

"Better mark it sixteen-minus."

The mayor laughed. "No, I think my algebra is all right."

When they finally got down to starting the formal hearing, the charge was read.

"Miss Wise, to the charge of maliciously and willfully shooting Jacob Kastanowitz, what do you plead?" Mayor Henry asked.

"I am not guilty," she replied.

Judge Lewis Brucker was called to the stand. He testified to the repeated lunacy hearings which resulted in Kastanowitz being sent off to either the asylum or the workhouse. Brucker claimed that afterward, upon returning to Mansfield, Kastanowitz would immediately return to bothering Phebe. He said that it was his understanding that Phebe would at times look out the window late and night and find Jake looking in.

T.F. Black, the mayor of Mansfield from 1893 to 1895, testified that he had advised Phebe for years to shoot Kastanowitz but that she was reluctant to actually do it. He said he knew of no woman who had been pursued so long and so relentlessly.

Katherine Friedgen, who lived in Fairview, testified that for some years, Kastanowitz had not held down a job.

"He wasn't an industrious man?" Henry asked.

"I never thought so," Friedgen replied.

Irene Funk was part of the group of women who had visited Phebe that Sunday. She testified to seeing Jake there.

"At first," Funk said, "he was along the road. Miss Wise had just been telling us how he had been acting during the day. I looked out and saw him. He had a large club in his hand."

Also part of the group was Addie Brooks. "I saw him standing in front of her house. He stood and looked in the door for about half an hour from the road and then came inside the yard. He hid in the bushes."

At last, Phebe's friend Gus Douglass was called to the stand.

"We used to arrest him, leave him there during a term of court, then indict him, leave him there for another term of court and then release him, as there seemed to be no place he could be sent. We would keep him in jail just as long as we dared and then let him go. I know no one who was so perpetually in trouble. Nothing did him any good. He was almost an unbearable burden to her. I would send him to jail, keep him there, remonstrate with him, talk to him, but it did no good."

Prosecutor Bowers asked Phebe if she wished to make a statement. After a brief whisper with Douglass and the other lawyers present, she declined.

Bowers turned to the mayor and spoke. "Miss Wise was at her home when the deed was done, and she had a right to protect herself. I therefore submit a motion that Miss Wise be discharged and that she be permitted to go hence without delay."

The mayor approved the motion, and the courtroom crowd broke out in a round of applause for Phebe Wise, who was cleared of all charges and free to go.

The coroner had held an inquest the same morning and come to the same conclusion of Phebe's act being a justifiable homicide.

Many editorials followed, pontificating that though Phebe Wise might be a touch eccentric in her clothing and manner, she was to be admired for protecting herself and her chastity. "Few women have the courage to remain alone in their own home for a whole night," the editor wrote, savoring his opportunity to beat his breast. "Let them try to imagine what it would be to pass night after night for weeks and months and years in some isolated cottage with a demoniacal creature of human form in physical construction only, prowling about the premises uttering vile as well as violent vows of adoration, and pleading for admittance, followed by threats of forcible invasion and personal violence."

Not one of the editorials called for a revision of the laws to prevent obsessive stalking. Almost one hundred years would pass before such laws were finally placed on the books (following the murder of television actress Rebecca Schaeffer in 1989).

Judge Lewis Brucker. *John Sherman Room, Mansfield Richland County Public Library.*

One curious footnote remains. In 1902, an audit of Judge Lewis Brucker's probate court records found that Brucker had, for almost a decade, been overcharging defendants involved in lunacy proceedings at the court. The findings were published in the newspaper, presumably so that those who had been overcharged could apply for refunds. Jacob Kastanowitz is listed four times in the report: December 21, 1891; August 10, 1892; September 6, 1893; and August 4, 1894. On each occasion, Brucker charged him fees that were more than double the legal limit; on the final occasion, he charged him almost triple. Jake had been overcharged $20.07, the equivalent of nearly $700 in 2023.

That's a steep overage for a low-paid factory worker to handle, especially after his mental condition made him unable to hold a job. There's no indication that Jake Kastanowitz realized this or cared, nor is there any record of his parents later collecting the difference. In fact, Eva Kastanowitz would only outlive her son by a few years, dying of heart failure on October 19, 1903.

Ironically, the frail John Kastanowitz would outlive his entire family and find himself alone in a country where he couldn't even speak the language. On Wednesday, May 31, 1905, Pennsylvania Railroad passenger train no. 403 was westbound through Mansfield. At the intersection of the tracks with East Fourth Street, railroad gates had already come down to warn of the approaching train. John either didn't notice the gates and the oncoming, whistling train, or he simply didn't care anymore. He stepped out onto the tracks in the path of the train and was immediately killed. In a carefully worded ruling, Richland County coroner Dr. Goodman stated that the deceased came to his death after being struck by the train. He avoided the use of the word *accident*, and he did not officially rule his death the result of suicide. His will in the Richland County Probate Court was clearly written for him by someone who was fluent in English. Even though the document gives his name as "John," he signed, in a shaky hand, "Kastanowitz, Johan." It says that any funds he had remaining after his debts were paid were to go to his caretaker, Andrew Johnson, a neighbor from Fairview who took him in after Eva's death; Johnson was also given nine dollars to dig John's grave. He received the house on Jefferson Street, as there was no one else to receive it. The file says, "No next of kin living in this country."

Jake Kastanowitz's unmarked grave in Mansfield Cemetery. *Author's collection.*

John and Eva were buried beside Jake and his sister Mary in unmarked graves in Mansfield Cemetery, coincidentally located almost exactly the same distance away from Phebe Wise's later grave as their homes had been in life.

8

THAT BOY'S A LITTLE TETCHED

Despite her status as an eccentric, Phebe Wise occasionally entertained friends and visitors, those who could deal with a woman of bold opinions and unconventional habits. She enjoyed lively conversation and playing the piano for guests. Even as she began showing serious signs of wear, Phebe still had the aura of class about her. She was sought by those who, by her estimation, weren't "limpets clinging to the rock of conformity."

She still had family in the area who were among her frequent visitors. One day in the summer of 1904, she was visited by her cousin Charley. Charley's and Phebe's grandfathers were brothers. Charley shared some of Phebe's philosophical turn, as well as her restlessness. He was known as a gregarious person who never met a stranger as he traveled the length and breadth of Richland County. He did that when he ran for office, after a string a various jobs failed to work out, including a position as a bank teller in downtown Mansfield.

Charley loved people, and he loved talking, but he didn't like routine. His pressing the flesh got him elected to a term as county treasurer, but the routine of the job didn't suit the restless man either. He spent hours taking his son on rides on the family's horse and buggy, daydreaming about how he'd love to have the money to buy some of the old farms in Richland County, fix them up, get them productive again, and sell them to young farmers.

On this particular day, Charley brought his son Lewis with him when he dropped in to visit "Cousin Phebe." As they pulled down toward Phebe's small house from the Olivesburg Road, Charley looked across the broad valley leading down into the Flats of Mansfield, where the noisy, smoke-belching factories crouched. He may well have drawn the boy's attention to them. He likely also noted the location of Phebe's already infamous guard horse Scottie.

Phebe's cousin Charlie Brumfield. *Ohio Department of Natural Resources, Malabar Farm State Park.*

As Charley and his son got down from the buggy, Phebe came out onto the porch and greeted them. Perhaps, like some of her other friends, Charley intended to buy some farm goods from Phebe. He would have known perfectly well that he could get them for less elsewhere, but it was a good excuse to direct a few coins Phebe's way. Since more than a decade had passed since her parents' deaths, the bulk of the money they had left Phebe was also gone. The boy asked if he could stay outside while they went to the kitchen to catch up, and he was allowed to stay on the porch.

As boys will do, little Lewis got bored and began poking around in the yard. Looking down the hillside, he noticed the enticing glimmer of water down at the spring. It wasn't that far away from the house, he reasoned, so he strolled through the yard, past Phebe's jungle of flowers, past the decrepit barn, and made his way down to the spring pond. At first, he walked on the stone wall that braced the hillside, but he found the lure of the water irresistible, and walked to the low edge of the pond, where he knelt in the grass. He reached his hands into the water, which was refreshingly crisp on this warm summer day. He cupped his hands and drank and then started playing by sailing twigs on the surface of the pond as if they were miniature ships.

Playing in the water, he didn't pay any particular attention, at first, to the sound of hoofbeats. Though Lewis lived on Third Street in Mansfield, just behind the grand estate of U.S. senator John Sherman, the boy was familiar with more rural settings, frequently visiting his grandfather's farm just west of Mansfield. Hoofbeats were a commonplace sound.

The crescendo of the hoofbeats impressed itself on the boy's attention, however. They were getting rapidly louder, because the horse was running toward him. That's when it snapped into the boy's mind what horse would

The retaining wall of the pond on Phebe's property. *Author's collection.*

be running around at Phebe Wise's place: Scottie, the guard horse, the horse that had reputedly been trained to attack anyone, especially boys, who ventured onto Phebe's property with mischief in mind. Neighborhood gossip was that the horse would rush the interloper, forcing him to stop, and then swiftly dispatch him with a brutal kick of its front legs. To a boy the size of Lewis, such a blow would be fatal.

Lewis stood and whirled around just as Scottie arrived, panting furiously, snorting angrily and showing his teeth. The boy held his breath in terror as he and the horse looked at each other, eye to eye. He didn't break the eye contact, fearing that the moment he did, the horse would bite him or, worse, kick him into the pond, where his father would later find his floating, dead body. For seemingly long minutes, the boy and the horse carefully eyed each other.

Disaster having not happened, Lewis found his heartbeat slowing as he looked at the magnificent animal. Young Lewis adored animals. It was a feeling that was only intensified by watching the wild and tame animals coursing around Phebe's place. One of the boy's favorite places to be was his grandfather's farm or alongside his father as he drove the buggy, talking about the ways he'd love to restore old broken-down farms that had lost their hearts. Animals, farms, and nature were central to the growing boy's world, and even an infamously cantankerous beast like Scottie attracted the boy. He wanted more than anything to reach out and pet the horse.

Noting that the horse had calmed as he held eye contact with it, Lewis slowly reached out, letting the horse sniff his hand while willing himself not to panic in fear of a bite. The horse softly whinnied, baring its teeth as if to remind the boy who he was, but he did not bite. The boy extended his hand a little farther and pet the horse's head as it bowed down, allowing him to do so. He began talking to the horse about how he loved animals and about the pond.

That gave Lewis an idea. He reached down, cupped his hands, and dipped them into the water. He slowly pulled up a dripping handful and offered it to Scottie. The horse drank the water from his hands and then reached down and drank more from the spring. The chatty boy resumed talking and idly splashed his hands in the water. The horse surprised him by nodding its head down briskly to splash the water, too.

Smiling, Lewis splashed the water again, and the horse matched him. Playing, they escalated their splashes until the boy got some water on the horse. Scottie reached his head down and sent a wave of water over the boy, who shrieked in laughter. The boy and horse started a full-blown water fight. By this point, Charley and Phebe had finished chatting in the kitchen and heard the ruckus. Charley came through the door and was about to break into a run when he saw the dreaded horse looming over his son.

Phebe quickly spoke up. "Well, I'll be," she said. "I have never seen Scottie play with a boy like that." After they watched the cavorting pair for a moment, Phebe became convinced that this child had the touch, that special ability some people have to connect with animals, nature, and the spiritual and otherworldly.

"That boy's a little tetched," she said. The boy turned and made eye contact with the witchlike old woman; a special bond that would last forever was immediately forged between them. He would later say that this image of her would follow him around the world, even causing him to dream of her at times.

The boy's father was Charles Brumfield, and the boy himself was Lewis Brumfield, who later Frenchified his first name and classed-up his last name to become Louis Bromfield, future Pulitzer Prize–winning author and conservationist. This account of that morning is my own fleshing out of Bromfield's brief retelling of it in his book *Pleasant Valley*. It marked the beginning of Bromfield's uncanny connection with Phebe Wise.

The eccentric woman proved to be one of the key formative influences on Bromfield, as he wrote about her and her world with the same tone of stricken awe that he reserved for nature elsewhere. And time and again, Phebe cropped up in his writings, and it was noted that each time a new Bromfield book came out, the publishers were instructed to send review copies to all the major literary critics and Miss Phebe Wise of Mansfield, Ohio. This tradition continued until Phebe's death.

As Bromfield was born in Mansfield in 1896, the horse encounter likely took place sometime around 1904, as Bromfield described himself as being seven or eight years old when it happened. This certainly matches the gradual decline of Phebe's fortunes, which many friends and acquaintances tried in small ways to help alleviate without offending the fiercely proud Phebe. She became a significant figure in the boy's world, though he didn't know her well. Nonetheless, her individuality and connection with nature gave her an authority that he granted few others in his life. For instance, while it is known that the young Lewis was driven hard by his mother, who was determined to see her children achieve more status in the world than her daydreaming husband, Nettie Brumfield was largely uncultured herself. The magnificently well-rounded young man who eventually emerged in literary circles owed his taste to the teachers who took a generous interest in the boy's education and his aspiration to be as perceptive as Phebe Wise.

Phebe had remained widely read and well-versed in art and music, and in her few encounters with Lewis, she must have impressed these perceptions and tastes onto the boy, who had a spongelike memory and a voracious appetite for all forms of the arts. But additionally, Lewis studied Phebe herself, noting her precarious position as an outsider who nonetheless managed to maintain a position of begrudging respect in the community. He saw how, quite literally, Phebe's position on the small farm overlooking Mansfield gave her a vantage point from which to observe the world of the small midwestern city. And she did it her own way in a time when many women with lesser eccentricities were shipped off to the state mental hospitals. She remained singular in a society of couples; she lived on a farm but ate no meat; she loved debating politics but never voted, remaining what Bromfield later termed a "Rousseau-like anarchist." Figuratively, Phebe's position as an eccentric gave her the perspective young Lewis wanted. The budding writer understood that in order to tell a story, you have to have a vantage point from which to observe. This led to his constant, obsessive jockeying for positions from which to observe and comment on the entire world, which led to his fame and lasting influence. In short, without Phebe Wise, there would never have been a Louis Bromfield.

The last time Bromfield saw Phebe was the day he was to leave Mansfield to go to Europe as part of the American Ambulance Corps, which was part of the fighting forces in France. Bromfield later wrote that he could still see Phebe dressed in a yellow taffeta dress with a bustle and wearing black lace gloves and cheap costume jewelry rings from the five and dime store on North Main Street. As Bromfield was boarding the train, he looked up the North Main Street hill. In the distance, he was able to spot Phebe Wise's outrageous image on the sidewalk outside Ashbrook's drugstore, pontificating to passers-by.

Lewis Brumfield goes to war. *Ohio Department of Natural Resources, Malabar Farm State Park.*

"I was glad that on the day I left for the war, the unearthly, witchlike Phoebe was almost the last person I saw," Bromfield wrote in *Pleasant Valley*.

He had no idea then that he'd never see her again.

After the war, Bromfield tackled New York City by becoming an editor for the Associated Press and writing music criticism for *Time* magazine. He worked the social circles hard and married Mary Appleton Wood, a socialite whose family was in the publishing business. He also wrote and discarded four novels, finding them inadequate attempts. But finally, he began to reach a level of writing that caught the attention of publishers and critics. He had arrived.

After Bromfield's first novel, *The Green Bay Tree*, was published in 1924 to great acclaim, Phebe Wise swam back into his thoughts, likely because he took considerable inspiration from his early years in Mansfield in the work and its successor, *Possession*. Between these two stately but deeply felt novels, he wrote the first version of a short story called "The Wedding Dress" for *Collier Magazine* in the fall of 1925. It later became known as "The Life of Zenobia White" and was published in Bromfield's short story collection *Awake and Rehearse*.

In the story, the narrator tells of a neighbor running up and breathlessly telling him that Zenobia White was dead. The neighbor is speechless after shouting his news, dimly aware that something significant has changed in the world. The narrator goes into his own thoughts:

Thus something had gone out of our little world. I should never see Zenobia White again walking with her fantastic disordered dress of yellow taffeta and black lace, trailing its long train in the dust of the highway, a basket over one arm, her black lace mitts adjusted neatly…walking down the highway, very tall and straight and proud, her black eyes flashing beneath the little veil of black lace that hung from the brim of her queer, bedraggled bonnet. . . .Zenobia White. . .immensely old, more than a hundred perhaps, who had lived, as far back as any of us could remember, in a little house covered with vines that stood behind a great barrier of bushes down by the covered bridge. Zenobia White, immensely fierce and old, who dressed always in yellow taffeta.

Then the narrator speaks specifically of Zenobia's almost supernatural connection to nature:

As far back as my father could remember, she had lived in the untidy old house. Animals came to her without fear. The very birds in her garden were tame. The thrushes and the cardinals abounded. In the cupola of her tiny house, there were whole colonies of martins. Stray dogs came to her…the stray dogs, yellow and spotted, without name or breed, who had howled on the morning when Zenobia had not come out to feed them. And cats were there, great numbers of cats who lived in peace with the dogs and who followed her in a grotesque procession a little distance down the road when she set out in the morning in the trailing gown of yellow taffeta to do her marketing.

This description made it astonishingly clear to any Mansfielder who read it, including Phebe Wise herself, who had inspired it. Bromfield later said that Phebe wasn't offended, finding it all rather amusing and, as far as the romance was concerned, completely outside her character. But it almost immediately began distorting stories of the old woman.

In the story, the dead woman's body is found decked out in a wedding dress so old that it has turned yellow with age. The reason she was wearing this wedding dress was because seventy years earlier, she had been engaged to be married to a young Scottish pioneer named Duncan McLeod. One evening, just days before their marriage, the two quarreled, befitting their volatile tempers, and Zenobia went home alone. She sat in her little house, reading the Bible and praying for God to chasten her temper, as she listened to the ghostly sound of owls. Around midnight, she heard a sound outside, and grabbing her gun, she shot through the door to defend herself from the intruder. The following morning, Zenobia discovered the dead body of Duncan McLeod outside her door. She has worn the wedding dress all these years in memory of the marriage that never happened.

The shooting of Duncan McLeod is obviously a romanticized version of Phebe's killing of Jake Kastanowitz, one that tries to explain away an elderly woman's eccentricity as a result of her inability to let herself be tamed by the man she loved. In that way, it is the kind of a sexist mistake Bromfield rarely made when writing about women, as he was known in his day as an unusually sympathetic writer of female characters—for a male, anyway—and thus, his fan base was known to be predominantly composed of women. That may well be one of the reasons Ernest Hemingway, the crown prince of toxic masculinity, could not stand Bromfield.

But the story does at least portray Zenobia's independence and individuality with unbowed integrity, something the real Phebe must have impressed on him. It would take more literary tries, though, before he truly captured her essence.

Meanwhile, the wedding dress element of the story subsequently grew to infiltrate many retellings of Phebe's own story, and her mother's old ball gowns were transmogrified into a mysterious wedding dress, suggesting some forlorn loss of love in her earlier days, something that does not, in fact, appear to have ever happened. No wonder Phebe was amused by the story. It only shares surface similarities to her own life. She surely must have had a grim sense of humor about it. Once again, here was a reason not to trust men. Her former protégé was now hijacking her story and turning it into romantic fiction. While she had tried to connect the boy to the seething depths of energy that lurk latently beneath the mundane surfaces of this world, he was largely missing it. Only in the narrator's sense that something tremendous has gone out of the world with Zenobia's passing does Bromfield show a grasp of Phebe Wise's values. It would take him years to get a better grip on them.

It is interesting to note that this gothic romance bears a passing resemblance to the famous William Faulkner story "A Rose for Emily." Interestingly, though, Bromfield's story came five years before Faulkner wrote his tragic tale of a lovelorn recluse. Faulkner's tale intensified the horror and became a classic, though Bromfield's story persisted for some time as one of his better-known pieces before receding into the mass of forgotten literature of the 1920s.

Bromfield's fame nonetheless grew throughout that period, culminating in him being awarded the Pulitzer Prize for his third novel, *Early Autumn*, in 1927. He was in demand everywhere and was hailed as one of the major authors of the day. Bromfield returned to Mansfield once in 1927 while on a whirlwind tour to give a speech at Mansfield Senior High School. At Phebe's advanced age, it is unlikely she attended, and if she had, surely, he would have noticed those black, snapping eyes, even in the back of the auditorium. Bromfield only had time to make a quick, depressing trip to his grandfather's farm, which, even then, was starting to be encroached on by the city. (Today, it is crisscrossed by highways.) Then Bromfield was back on the road, the busy celebrity tending to his fame. Perhaps in his mind, thanks to what he had written, Phebe Wise was already a fixture of the past, even though she was still alive at that time. If that was the case, she clearly still haunted him.

After taking inspiration from his own wife for his fourth novel, *A Good Woman*, Bromfield wrote an ambitious fifth novel, *The Strange Case of Miss Annie Spragg*. While not a direct portrait of Phebe Wise—and with its Italian setting nowhere near Mansfield—some elements of Phebe's personality show up in the distinctive titular character. And the work's ambition to

Louis Bromfield, a successful writer. *Ohio Department of Natural Resources, Malabar Farm State Park.*

91

unite themes of love and spirituality suggests Bromfield was still trying to improve his grasp of the kind of deep philosophical ideas Phebe had kindled in him.

Throughout the late 1920s and early 1930s, Bromfield was globetrotting. He wrote unhappily for a spell in Hollywood before buying out his contract. Then he relocated to France and became a prominent part of the American expatriate scene there. But after clawing his way to the top of literary fame, Bromfield found the work hollow. He called the upper-class crowd of dissipated celebrities and penniless royals the "international white trash set" and began portraying them negatively in his books, which began the turn of his literary reputation in those powerful circles.

While still hosting Sunday brunches at his house in Senlis, France (that might last from Thursday to Tuesday), Bromfield began to grow bored with celebrity and literary fame. At the same time, he was accumulating household members, including his parents, who needed to be supported, as well as a business manager, George Hawkins, who moved in and became his amanuensis. This necessitated a move to more mainstream writing—and people loved his scathing portraits of the elites—resulting in his shift to a more popular focus, aiming for the best-seller market.

Meanwhile, though, Bromfield watched from a distance as American agriculture collapsed during the Dust Bowl. He had himself been carrying considerable guilt over chasing fame while his family lost their farm in the late 1910s. This began to come out as longing memories of his grandfather's farm as Bromfield began gardening in Senlis. All this reflection on cultivation led him, in 1932, to write *The Farm*, taking its inspiration from his family's roots in Richland County, Ohio. And turning back to his childhood inevitably brought Bromfield back to Phebe Wise.

This time, he got closer to the essence of Phebe, who was still alive at the time of the writing. In this piece, she becomes the character Zenobia van Essen, but her description is still unmistakable: "Zenobia van Essen lived in a house outside the Town which stood in the shadow of the hard gray walls of the State Prison."

He describes her garden as a tangle of flowers gone wild, including honeysuckle, wisteria, and eglantine. Bromfield savors her sprawling garden and the tame and wild animals running through it, interacting with Zenobia and swimming in the spring pond.

The mythologizing of Phebe continues as he describes her character as "well past seventy," though at the time Bromfield himself first saw Phebe, she was little more than fifty. Her stresses had aged her prematurely. He describes his character Zenobia as being the great-granddaughter of a Wyandot chief, which seems to echo the distant possibility of Phebe's connection to Chief Tom Jelloway, one of the last Natives in the area in the early nineteenth century, as discussed in chapter 3. Bromfield describes Zenobia as having bronze skin, high cheekbones, and an erect posture, all supposed to be Native traits.

This time around, he fleshes out the portrait of Zenobia by describing her as being isolated from her own family by her own hauteur and also as someone willing to file a lawsuit at the drop of a hat, both of which match quite tidily to what is known of Phebe. In place of a simple love story with a tragic turn, Bromfield delivers a relationship much closer to what really happened between Phebe and Jake Kastanowitz. He even gives this introduction to the obsessive suitor: "One of them, a young man called Zachariah Betts, showed an unusual ardor. He would not be dismissed, and when she would no longer open the door to him he came at night to wander about the garden, calling out his admiration and attempting now and then to force the shutters."

Zachariah Betts attempts to force his way into Zenobia's house one night, and she shoots him through the door, finding his dead body in the morning. Bromfield also describes how Zenobia weathers the subsequent arraignment and becomes interested in the workings of the law. This time, Bromfield sees beyond the melodrama of his character's life and recognizes her struggle: "In a way, her tragedy was that of a woman born at the wrong time. She had intelligence and independence and great force of character, but in her day and situation, there was nothing left for her to do but become an eccentric and to end her life as the prey of small boys who came to the cottage to torment her and the old white horse."

Coming back to the figure of Phebe Wise and engaging with his rural roots stirred something deep in Louis Bromfield, a calling to return to his homeland and do something practical to help the world through farming, for, as one of his characters in *The Farm* says, "Some day there will come a reckoning and the country will discover that farmers are more necessary than traveling salesmen, that no nation can exist or have any solidity which ignores the land. But it will cost the country dear. There'll be hell to pay before they find it out."

Phebe Wise died before *The Farm* was published. Bromfield was away in India at the time and did not hear about her death until later. But as the ghost of memory, Phebe was even stronger. She and her world, just tantalizingly out of reach, were pulling Bromfield back to Ohio. By the late 1930s, as war loomed like thunder on the European horizon, Bromfield left France and returned to the United States.

After searching for a suitable farm site on the East Coast, Bromfield returned to Ohio. His searches led him back to the north-central part of the state, an area he had visited years before with his father, Charley. Seeing the area made Bromfield's heart leap, and he immediately got out of his car and made a generous cash offer to farmer Clem Herring to buy his house and land. He added other properties to it, including the old miller's house that was an infamous part of the Ceely Rose murders, and collectively called the place Malabar Farm, inspired by the Malabar Coast of India.

The farm was located in Pleasant Valley in the southeast corner of Richland County. With it, Louis Bromfield wanted to lead the way to a new approach to agriculture, something sustainable and restorative. It became his passion project of the rest of his life, and it is the core that his fame rests on today, because despite his variable successes and occasional outright errors, Bromfield did spark a movement in sustainable agriculture that continues today. He began writing articles, speeches, and radio shows on the subject, spreading his fame to the point that the Truman administration even vetted him as a possible candidate to be the secretary of agriculture.

By the time Malabar Farm was forming, many of Bromfield's stories were being made into Hollywood films, which helped sponsor the enormous cost of Malabar Farm. And there was still demand for more books, so Bromfield kept writing. But something new emerged in 1944 with the publication of the short story collection *The World We Live In*. In it, one can sense an acceleration in the author's distancing of himself from high society and further exploring his rural roots. He skewers the "international white trash" mercilessly in "A Death in Monte Carlo" via the character Mrs. Pulsifer, who, perhaps not coincidentally, seems like a close cousin of Phebe Wise, wittily disdaining the nonsense of the fools around her rushing to oblivion. But the main event of the collection, without question, is the story "Up Ferguson Way." It stands as Bromfield's most noble portrait of Phebe and as a source of confusing complications to those not familiar with Phebe's true story.

Bromfield starts the story with an interesting literary device. He is clearly narrating in the first person, setting up what appears to be the tone of memoir. But it isn't. This is actually another piece of fiction, though it is one with a great deal of personal memory invested. He starts off by saying that he has written of a grand woman from his childhood twice before while she was still alive. He has invented the names Zenobia White and Zenobia Van Essen to protect her privacy. In this story, however, he says that he will reveal her "real name" now that she is dead. But he does not say her name is Phebe Wise, because he's not writing a memoir.

Instead, Bromfield embarks on a clever literary journey, combining two important, real stories from his life into an imaginary plot. Bromfield's favorite place on his Malabar property was the old Ferguson meadow. It lies on the ridge overlooking the valley and had been the site of John Ferguson's farm. Most of the early settlers of the Pleasant Valley area set up farms in the valley at a sociable distance from one another. The Fergusons chose the remote top of the ridge, seemingly as far away from the other settlers as possible. With the land here being less rich than the valley bottom lands, the Ferguson farm was likely more hardscrabble, but the family survived. John Ferguson and two of his sisters lived out their lives there and left behind a small house.

Bromfield found the high meadow near the old Ferguson homestead to be a haven of escape. Whenever the world was too much for him, Bromfield would hop in his Willys Jeep and climb the dirt road up the ridge. In time, going "up Ferguson way," became code that meant he needed to be left alone to think and contemplate. If a Bromfield family member or employee encountered another in the Ferguson meadow, they let them be. It was a sacred space that was remote, close to the sky and quiet.

Wanting to wrap this place into his continuing obsession with Phebe Wise, Bromfield combined the two in the story "Up Ferguson Way." He "reveals" that the supposed real name of the woman from his childhood was not Zenobia White or Van Essen, but it was actually Zenobia Ferguson. He then proceeds to transfer Phebe Wise and her curious little house to Ferguson meadow. It is here, in connecting the idea of Phebe with his own green cathedral, that Bromfield taps the depths of what Phebe meant to him:

> *The longer I live the more I am inclined to believe in forces which we do not understand, which compel our destinies along other courses from those we have carefully planned. I can't help believe too that these same forces entangle our lives with those of theirs, although they may be strangers or persons only encountered casually two or three times in all our lives. Something like that happened with Zenobia's life and mine. I never knew her very well for she was already an old woman when I was born and I saw her only casually in my youth, but in a life spent largely wandering about the earth in meeting thousands of people of every race, nationality and creed I never met one who left upon me so profound an impression.*

He then tells the story of traveling by buggy with his father to visit Zenobia when he was seven or eight years old. While Charley disappears inside the house, the boy wanders down to Zenobia's spring pond to play with and observe the animals:

> *The cow came down to the pond to drink, the new calf teetering on its long legs, moving forward in jerky sudden movements. I stopped digging to watch and suddenly the calf became my brother, a small creature for whom I felt a sudden intense love, quite different from the sort of love I felt for any person, even my own parents or my brothers or sisters. It was as if we were both a part of something which other people did not understand, a whole world apart in which there were sounds which no human could understand. I knew suddenly what the ducks were quacking about and understood the look in the great brown eyes of the Jersey cow.*

As the boy communes with the animals in his spiritual awakening, he senses someone is watching him. He turns around to see Zenobia Ferguson peering at him, smiling. "[S]uddenly I had for her the same fathomless understanding," Bromfield writes.

A squirrel then jumps onto Zenobia's arm and bounds up her arm and onto her shoulder. "He's teched like us," she explains. Soon, Charley wanders back down from the house, spoiling the reverie, but it doesn't matter. The boy's life has been forever changed by this encounter with nature and the shamanistic figure intertwined with it.

Bromfield then fleshes out the story with a retelling of the early, romantic version of Zenobia shooting her lover through the door, but it feels like a footnote here. He then draws back into the contemplative view of the old woman, who somehow lives on.

This reengagement with Bromfield's lodestone did not exorcise her from his thoughts. Just a year later, he finally revealed his inspiration in his book of nonfiction essays *Pleasant Valley*. In the chapter "On Being 'Teched,'" he's almost apologetic for returning to this figure again. "Indeed," he writes, "I have written so frequently of her that at times I have very nearly worn out the subject, like an etching plate which has grown old and worn from use." He again describes Phebe's distinctive garb, this time adding that mud and dust had discolored her dress up to about knee level.

His description of her place focuses, as always, on the jungle-like garden, suggesting that in some way, Phebe's garden stood symbolically for the creative force of the universe itself, resisting excessive control, always running toward freedom. For all his instinctive understanding of that idea, Bromfield had tremendous trouble with actually letting go in his writing and his often-turbulent family relationships. So, the image nagged him:

> *It was a tiny house with a small turret and a great many tiny gables and much fretwork, overgrown, rotting and forced apart by the thrusting shoots of wisteria and trumpet vine. The little garden which surrounded it was a jungle of old-fashioned flowers—lilacs, mock orange, day lilies, petunias and a hundred other shrubs and plants. Here she lived alone surrounded by all sorts of animals, both wild and tamed. Between them and her there existed an extraordinary relationship. She allowed no hunter on or near her place and she had been known to drive them away on more than one occasion with an old-fashioned musket. Although it was doubtful whether the rusty musket could have done anyone the least harm, she carried the prestige of once having shot and killed a man, and trespassers did not pause to argue with her. Her only guardian was not a dog but an old white horse which she had raised from a colt without once having harnessed or bridled it. The old horse would run at trespassers, showing his teeth and kicking out viciously with his forefeet. You could not enter the place unless she called off the horse which obeyed her exactly as if it had been a watchdog.*

After a perfunctory mention of the story of Phebe Wise killing an unwanted suitor in self-defense, Bromfield tells the story of his encounter with the horse in a single paragraph, which I attempted to flesh out in the opening of this chapter.

Bromfield himself makes the connection between Johnny Appleseed and Phebe Wise:

> *Both of them have become legends in our country because they represented something which all men and women at some time envy and seek to attain—that poverty, that simplicity, that richness which is the essence of true Christian teaching and experience and far above all worldly riches. In a way the two of them acquired, like St. Francis, that intimacy with God and with Nature and birds and animals, that lack of all envy or ambition or greed, which is the ultimate "oneness with God." That is why they have become not only legends but in a way saints of our countryside.*

Bromfield writes that they will be remembered long after the millionaires, politicians and great manufacturers are forgotten.

One final time, Bromfield reprised "On Being 'Teched'" in his anthology *Animals and Other People* in 1955, less than a year before his own death. He reprinted the essay but added some closing thoughts:

> *For so long as the land is rich, the sunlight shines and the moon comes out, there is no need for man to be either poverty-stricken or miserable. The roots of his failure come not from the past nor even from the present but from within himself, out of his egotism, his envy, his laziness, his selfishness, his self-pity, his isolation from all that can make of a life a colorful and satisfactory existence. He has all the universe in which to live, and all of Nature to delight and comfort him and good honest work to give him strength and his reason for existence. What more could one ask of paradise?*
>
> *All that was, I think, part of the wisdom of old Phoebe Wise in her gown of soiled and dusty yellow taffeta and her jewels from Woolworth's.*

Whatever arguments can be made with Bromfield's philosophy, it was an influential one that influenced later figures like poet Wendell Berry and conservationist Wes Jackson, both of whom have cited Bromfield as a key influence. And as written previously, Bromfield clearly traced his own roots back to Phebe Wise.

9

THE WITCH OF MANSFIELD

E ven as early as 1897, Mansfield's view of Phebe had been captured in an article a *Richland Shield and Banner* reporter wrote after a spontaneous interview with Phebe on a streetcar.

She is rather an eccentric character and her oddities as regard to her apparel causes her to be a cynosure for all eyes, whenever she appears in public. She has a fondness for bright colors and never fails to wear the brightest of them and incidentally, as many as possible.

Notwithstanding her rather odd tastes in the matter of dress, Miss Wise is not an ignorant woman by any manner of means. In fact she is very intelligent, even if she is decidedly eccentric. She is possessed of considerable property, her wealth is variously estimated anywhere from $10,000 to $100,000. She is not what might be termed a handsome woman, being nearly six feet tall and of a muscular build. Her eyes, deepset, are black as midnight and seem to pierce one through and through. She is not exactly a stylish woman. She doesn't believe in bangs, frills and the like, and her long straight black hair has never felt the sizzling of the curling iron so much in vogue. Her hands are large and broad and show evidences of hard work and plenty of it. She cultivates a few acres and does all the work herself.

The reporter gave a perfect example of the myth building around Phebe in his statement that it was thought Phebe's wealth was somewhere between $10,000 and $100,000 in value. The truth was that the Wise property had been valued at only $3,000 when Phebe inherited it. That and whatever cash her parents had left her was all the wealth Phebe had to live on for the rest of her life unless she went back to work as a schoolteacher or took on some other sort of trade. Considering that she outlived her parents by over forty years, it's easy to see how she fell on hard times in her later years, especially if the reports about her spending habits are accurate.

In the 1890s, she still had enough money to make shopping trips into downtown Mansfield and return home laden with packages on the trolley. She was on such an expedition when the reporter quoted previously encountered her on the Diamond Street line.

"Are you doing your Christmas shopping, Miss Wise?" he asked her.

"Yes," Phebe said. "You see, I have to buy my own Christmas presents, and therefore, I buy just as many as I want."

The reporter was nonplussed. "It seems to me that when you have so many things to buy, you would come to the city in your carriage instead of being compelled to carry so many bundles."

"Well, you see," she said, looking down at the train of her mud-splattered dress, "I didn't care about getting the whole family splashed up, and anyway, my pony is getting so awful wild."

"Your whole family?"

"Yes, my pony, my buggy, and myself constitute my family, you know," Phebe said. The reporter said that she then smiled grimly. In typical fashion, she then decided to reverse the interrogation.

"Say, what do you think of lawyers?" she said.

The reporter, unaccustomed to being on the receiving end of an interview, babbled out something about figuring lawyers were a pretty good class of people.

"Well, I'll tell you what I think," Phebe said. "I think they're all a lot of schemers and tricksters. I guess I ought to know, for haven't I had enough experiences with them, goodness knows."

Phebe's dealings with officials of all stripes were often fraught. When the streetcar line had originally been built from Diamond Street to the then-new reformatory, the rail company asked Phebe for a slight easement onto her property to allow sufficient room for the tracks. Phebe angrily refused, saying that she'd give them that right-of-way only if they paid her the $1 million her property was worth.

The rail company of course refused. For years afterward, Phebe claimed that the streetcar company came during the night and moved her fence back a couple of feet to allow for its tracks. Most people dismissed Phebe's

The railroad tracks leading into Mansfield. A streetcar used to run alongside these tracks between downtown Mansfield and the Ohio State Reformatory. *Author's collection.*

claim as the exaggerated ravings of a crazy lady, but when neighbor John Van Cura Jr. had the property surveyed many years later, he discovered, to his shock, that the real property line actually sat a couple of feet into the railroad bed. The easement had indeed been stolen by a company that was certain that no one would pay that much attention to an eccentric old woman.

It was widely noted that Phebe lived in greater solitude as the years passed, retreating from the world into her books and music, which suited her fine. Marji Hazen wrote about her property: "The house was beginning to show its age. Phoebe was growing old as well and could not care for things as she had when young.…[U]ndergrowth crept over the once closely cropped lawn, climbed the gnarled old trees and choked out the flower beds." While some were no doubt irritated by Phebe, many embraced her as the town's most colorful character. To help feed herself, she had, for many years, kept chickens, but the birds were left to forage for themselves, which caused some tension with the neighbors, whose gardens the chickens would regularly raid. She also had a posse of barn cats running about the place and had tamed the squirrels in her yard to eat out of her hand. As the years went by, her guard horse Scottie grew thinner and thinner.

Her neighbor John Van Cura provided a description of the house around 1910:

> *The living room was just a little nook here and there. If there was a square corner, she'd have to put something in to knock it off—one of those corner closets or something like that that. Under the rugs that looked like paisley shawls she'd have a lot of broken boxes tramped down to make a kind of cushion. Every once in a while a rat would come out of there. When we'd get set down again and start talking, pretty soon we'd hear a racket in the breadbox and there'd be a rat working on her cookies. She'd take them out, tuck them under her arm and she'd say, "The darn thing won't let nothing alone." Then she'd start eating them rat-chewed cookies.*
>
> *She had a little pot-bellied stove that she'd cook beans on. She'd have the things goin' and every once in a while they'd boil dry and she'd add more water. She never stirred the pot, just add water. When she'd have that pot of beans cooked and they'd be ready to serve, she'd look down in the bottom and they'd all be black.*

The fact that Phebe had once had money was suggested by Van Cura's comment that Phebe's favorite chair was a Heywood-Wakefield wicker chair, a popular furniture manufacturer during the turn of the century. By the time Van Cura was visiting her house, though, the wicker seat was broken, and Phebe had layers of various materials in place to plug the hole. He said that she loved her coffee and had a peculiar manner of getting a cup ready. She would grab her cup, pour a little coffee in it, slosh it around to rinse it—in a manner of speaking—and then fling it out. Then she'd pour a full cup to drink while talking. She'd continue this method until the entire pot of coffee was gone.

After the traumas Phebe experienced in the 1890s, her circle of friends grew small and select. Until she knew and trusted someone, she would be aloof and cold toward them. Once a person was trusted, though, she'd show her friendly and talkative side. With friends, she'd display her wit and sense of humor. It is said that she loved to discuss politics and current events.

While they were more sedate, Phebe's later years were not without their misadventures. One evening in mid-November 1911, she arrived home on the streetcar from downtown after dark. She followed her usual routine of

A double-exposure photograph of Phebe Wise and friends, circa 1930. *John Sherman Room, Mansfield Richland County Public Library.*

stopping at the barn before going into the house to check on Scottie. When she entered, the horse seemed agitated and came immediately to her. He rubbed his nose against her and nibbled at her.

In years of working closely together, Phebe and Scottie had worked out some means of communication. She knew immediately that something was wrong, because the nibbling was something Scottie only did when he was trying to communicate alarm to Phebe. It was a signal for trouble.

Phebe immediately picked up the nearest object she could use as a weapon—a piece of metal gas pipe—and crept to the door of the barn. Carefully, she looked out. Her own yard was dark, but there was a touch of illumination coming from the outdoor security lamps of the nearby Ohio State Reformatory. She stepped out into the yard and saw a shadowy figure skulking behind the hen house. She threw the pipe at the intruder.

The pipe didn't seem to faze him, and he started walking toward her. She reached back into the barn and grabbed a pitchfork. Brandishing her new weapon, she dared the man to come closer. He changed his mind about approaching her and stepped back into the darkness. She said that if he didn't like the pitchfork, he should wait around while she got another weapon for him to try.

She rushed into the house and went upstairs to fetch her shotgun. Looking out the window, Phebe caught a glimpse of a flashlight. As she looked at the light, she could see not one but two men running across the field, profiled in the dim security light from the reformatory. Phebe later told a newspaper reporter that she had her shotgun gauged to shoot for six hundred yards and thought she might be able to hit at least one of the fleeing burglars if they hadn't made such a quick getaway.

Phebe's next trip downtown included a stop to purchase a revolver, as a shotgun was "unhandy to carry around."

As the political issue of women's suffrage began to pick up momentum in the early years of the twentieth century, it was inevitable that the boldly independent Phebe's opinion would be sought out, as a reporter did in 1914.

"Would I vote if I was given the chance?" she rhetorically repeated the reporter's question. "Well, now, you just watch me once and see. I haven't spent the past twenty-five years of my life wrestling with crooked politicians and scheming lawyers without seeing the urgent need of a few good, clean-minded women in public affairs."

In 1917, Phebe was apparently interviewed by *Mansfield News Journal* reporter Jane Williams about the then infamous shooting of Jake Kastanowitz. Surprisingly, some of the details given differ from what was reported in 1898.

Williams states that, according to Wise, Kastanowitz was shot through the front door of the house. Perhaps this was in reference to the earlier shooting when Phebe winged Jake on the arm and sent him running. Either Williams or Phebe herself mixed up the two events, as there's a wealth of reporting from 1898 indicating that she shot him through the kitchen window.

One time, she became furious at the newspaper for printing rumors about her death.

"Now, don't you put it in the paper that I'm dead," she warned a reporter over the telephone. "I am feeling fine. They have all sorts of stories going about me. You can tell them I am all right." The rumors started in January 1918, during a particularly bitter winter. Phebe had been taken in by the Van Curas for several days, because they knew she was out of coal to heat her house. The resulting lack of activity around Phebe's house started the rumors. She told the reporter that she never knew she was so popular until she saw her picture in the paper, but then she scolded him for his choice of photograph.

Reports of Scottie's imminent demise started appearing in the late 1910s, but it wasn't until 1923 that his end came. The horse, just past his thirty-third birthday, had developed increasing difficulties walking thanks to arthritis, and on the morning of March 14, 1923, Phebe found him completely unable to rise from the ground. Distraught, she knew the time had come.

By this time, even the old-fashioned Phebe Wise had a telephone, and she used it to call Superintendent Jenkins at the neighboring reformatory. She begged him for help, asking him if he could come over and put poor Scottie out of his misery. Jenkins said that regulations would prevent him from doing anything directly, but he said he would procure some help for her immediately. Jenkins contacted the police and explained the situation. Patrolman Joe Adams was sent out to mercifully dispatch the poor animal, who had done a fine job protecting Phebe from what could have been many more incidents than the ones she already experienced. Phebe was, of course, devastated to lose her beloved guardian.

In 1926, Phebe suffered the further loss of her roly-poly, black, curly-haired dog. One by one, her closest friends were departing the world, leaving Phebe even more isolated. Mansfielders felt pity for her but found themselves uncertain of how to help.

According to Marji Hazen, the community would occasionally get swept up in a big project to help Phebe out, but that didn't always work. One time, the notion was that money could be raised to move Phebe to a life of comfort in a rest home. The old woman angrily refused the offer, still tenaciously holding to her father's insistence that the Wise property and its springs were of priceless value.

Phebe kept receiving copies of Louis Bromfield's latest books. He later commented that she was greatly amused by some of the flights of fiction that he took inspired by one detail or another of Phebe's life. That impression appears to have been conveyed to Bromfield by mutual friends, as there is no record of any correspondence between the writer and his muse. Though Bromfield once returned to Mansfield in 1927 to give a speech, there is no record that Phebe made it to the event. If she had, Bromfield would likely have spotted her distinctive figure and remarked on her presence.

On one occasion, a lawyer was her ally, but it was the end of a story that took decades to unfold. At one point in the late 1890s, Phebe showed up at the Sturges Bank in Mansfield, carrying a cigar box with a little bit of money in it. "I'm afraid someone will steal this money," she said. "Put it up for me, will you?" The teller promised to do so, but after Phebe left, she and the other bank workers had a good laugh about the box, all agreeing that the way Phebe spent money, she'd be back to empty it in no time at all. They put it on top of the steel safe and forgot about it.

In 1929, the New York Stock Market collapsed, bringing about the Great Depression. Banks all over the United States suffered sudden runs of depositors, causing the failures of many financial institutions, the Sturges Bank among them. The 1929 tellers had to break the news to Phebe Wise when she showed up, demanding her money. There had already been a run on the bank; they were out of cash.

"Sorry, Miss Wise," the teller said. "But there just isn't any money for you or anyone."

Phebe's sharp eyes searched the teller's face and then cast about, looking behind the counter at the walls and equipment. She spotted something on top of the safe, covered with years of cobwebs.

"My money is here, and I'm going to get it," Phebe said. She turned on her heel, stomped out of the bank and walked to the office of her lawyer, Howard Dirlam. Phebe and the lawyer returned to the Sturges Bank, stepladder in hand. The lawyer walked past the tellers and, without a word, set the stepladder down beside the safe and climbed it. He retrieved the cigar box from the top of the safe. They wiped the dust and cobwebs off the box and opened it to confirm that Phebe's money was still there.

The bank manager rushed out of his office indignantly.

"Here, now, that money will have to go to pay bank debts like all other deposits," he said.

The lawyer pointed out that the money had never actually been formally deposited, nor was it placed in a safety deposit box, and therefore, Phebe was entitled to take it back. She took it and left. In the economy of the day, it's safe to say the money didn't last her very long.

Phebe didn't suffer the mockery of children. In 1977, Virgil A. Stanfield interviewed Mansfield resident George W. Rowe, who grew up in a house just north of the reformatory during Phebe's later years. Rowe said that he was aware of her love for the piano and the banjo, so he decided to stop by one day to ask her to play him some music. Phebe was receptive to the request.

"She had covers over the piano," Rowe recalled, "But she removed them carefully, sat down, rubbed her fingers as if to make them more limber and came down on the keys with a tremendous crash. The piano was badly out of tune, and the sound was frightening."

Young Rowe laughed out loud at the wild cacophony, which infuriated Phebe. She jumped up and pulled the covers over the piano.

"Don't you ever ask me to play for you again," she snapped. The boy fled.

The superintendent of the neighboring Ohio State Reformatory tried to keep an eye on Phebe, delivering her care packages from time to time. Her neighbors, the Van Curas and others, also cared for Phebe, taking her in during some cold winters. In 2005, I spoke with a woman who lived in one of the homes where Phebe was taken in during a sharp winter in the early 1930s. She said that she didn't remember much about Phebe except that for hours on end, the old woman would sit in a rocking chair by the window and watch the birds, people, and weather. She remembered the woman's piercing eyes and said that she was very kind. But she said she also remembered avoiding Phebe, because one thing the old woman didn't do very often in her later years was take a bath. The current owner of that house told me that Phebe scratched her name into the wood of the windowsill she sat by and that, as of 2005, it was still there.

Adelia Hautzenroeder of Mansfield told me in 2005 about her memories of Phebe. She was told by her mother, who was the salad girl at Avery's Cafeteria on Fourth Street in Mansfield, that Mrs. Avery was protective of Phebe. When she would stop there for lunch, Mrs. Avery would find her the most isolated table in the restaurant so that she wouldn't be scrutinized by the public passersby. The cafeteria was located where the City Grille sits today.

While those who disliked Phebe may have been the first to call her a witch, there were those who believed it was true, especially children.

Dorothy Duckworth as old Phebe in the historical drama *Phoebe. Author's collection.*

"Of course, I was one of the believers that she was spooky," Adelia Hautzenroeder said. "It is just a faint recollection, but when we [Hautzenroeder and her brother] would pass her house, which was out by the reformatory, we'd make a big deal of our hurry to get by."

In 2005, I spoke briefly with Glenn Schroff, an eighty-eight-year-old gentleman who had attended one of the performances of my play *Phoebe.* He told me that as a child in Mansfield, around 1927 or 1928, he was a Boy Scout. One of the projects his troop did was to make up fruit baskets and distribute them to the poor people in town.

While delivering the baskets, the Boy Scouts came to the next person on their list: Phebe Wise. He told me that they all knew perfectly well who she was and that she was a familiar sight walking along the streets. Interestingly, though earlier accounts describe Phebe as being nearly six feet tall, Mr. Schroff remembered her as a short woman. Perhaps this is due to the pronounced stoop Phebe was said to have developed as a result of the abuse the robbers had heaped on her. Schroff did say that he remembered Phebe's big, flamboyant, flowery hat vividly.

The group of Boy Scouts stood there, staring at Phebe's house. They started telling each other to go deliver the basket. Each refused, the general drift of whispered discussion being that it was dangerous to step up to Phebe's door because she was an actual witch. Who knows what she might do to them.

The boys knew that they'd get in trouble if they skipped Phebe or just threw away the basket, so it was finally determined that, one way or another, they had to deliver the package. It was finally decided that the youngest scout should be the one to deliver the basket. After all, as the youngest, he was the most expendable. At the age of twelve, the youngest happened to be the man telling me the story over seventy-five years later. Glenn was entrusted with the basket, and though he was so scared he was trembling, he quickly walked through the yard to her porch. He placed the basket down and didn't even dare to knock on the door, lest the witch jump out and get him. He ran as fast as he could back to his friends, who congratulated him on his bravery. They left without lingering.

I like to imagine that Phebe was watching the entire scenario from behind a tattered curtain in her home, chuckling grimly to herself.

I also spoke with Louis Bromfield's youngest daughter, Ellen Bromfield Geld, on a number of occasions. She told me that Phebe Wise fascinated her as the old woman had fascinated her father. She said that Phebe and her fictional doubles were among her favorite characters in all her father's books. She was glad to hear of the dramas I was writing, conjuring up figures of the past to walk again.

Even in her final years, Phebe cut a striking figure, according to Marji Hazen, who said that even as late as 1930, Phebe would wear silk hoopskirts that swept the sidewalks and wide leghorn hats that had last been fashionable around the time of the Civil War. She decorated her hats copiously with bows and seasonal flowers, the flowers replaced in winter by sprigs of wheats or oats. She wore a scarf or a crepe paper bow to cover up the goiter she had on her neck that made it difficult for her to breathe and sleep. With her unwashed hands and face and general odor, Hazen said that behind her back, people would call Phebe "the pig." Hazen also said that Wise packed a pistol on her for self-defense ever since her days of robbers and mad suitors.

But Phebe Wise couldn't defend herself against the march of time.

Newspapers at the time supposed Wise was ninety-three years old or older, due to how long she had appeared old to the people of Mansfield. However, it should be remembered that trauma—of which Phebe experienced a great deal—can prematurely age a person's body. According to the best available reports, it is likely that Phebe was somewhere between her early to mid-eighties at the time of her death. She was buried in the Wise family plot in Mansfield Cemetery, but there was no money left for a headstone. Today, her grave is marked with a small photograph in order to identify the spot for those curious about Phebe's final resting place.

In the most controversial paragraph of her report on Wise, Marji Hazen gives a startling description of what the old woman's caretakers supposedly found as they prepared the body for the funeral: "[Phebe died]…in her old rope bed attended by neighbor women who gently cleaned away the grime of many years to reveal underneath the tan of many summers and the layers of faded old-fashioned clothes a skin not copper but white as any other Caucasian skin, still scarred by the tortures of long ago." Whether there's any truth to the report, it proves nothing one way or the other about the possible ethnic background of Phebe Wise. Rather, it is positive evidence of the racist attitudes that influenced some people's perception of Phebe.

Phebe's grave in the Wise family plot at Mansfield Cemetery. *Author's collection.*

Worse than the racism was the continued persistence of the legend of Phebe's wealth. After her death, the old house was slowly but surely picked apart by treasure hunters hoping to find hidden gold or something else of comparable value. While Phebe had sold off most of her parents' furniture over the years to help raise money to support herself, a few pieces remained and were quickly carted off. Others grabbed photographs and personal mementos, some of which still remain in the Mansfield area. One playgoer in 2005 showed me a glass bead necklace that was one of the many made from the bead shawl Phebe used to wear in her final years.

The *Mansfield News Journal* reported that police discovered the floor of the house covered with shredded books after treasure seekers tore apart Phebe's collection, looking for hidden money. A French bisque doll that Phebe had treasured since childhood was similarly disemboweled.

Reports state that the attic of the Wise house was full of moth-eaten buffalo robes, scout uniforms of dried-up buckskin that had once belonged to her brother, old hoopskirts, and crumbling books. An ancient bolt of Chinese silk was shattered to fragments as soon as it was moved.

John Van Cura boarded up the windows of the house to keep further vandals out. He was amazed to see a stream of cars from Cleveland and other Ohio cities driving by to see the house where Phebe Wise, who inspired Louis Bromfield's story "The Wedding Dress," had, until recently, lived. Many of them stopped and begged to be let inside the house, though Van Cura refused.

Phebe left no will and no immediate family. The probate court received inquiries from next of kin. One, Dessie Sturges of North Fairfield, Ohio, was said to be a cousin. Georgia Wise of Dunkirk, Ohio, claimed to be a niece, while William O. Cline of Los Angeles, California, wrote, claiming to be Phebe's nephew. If they thought there was anything to be inherited, they were out of luck.

Marion F. Cline was appointed the administrator of Phebe's estate, and appraisers were brought in. While they valued Phebe's remaining possessions at only $50, it appears that Christian Wise wasn't entirely wrong in saying that there was value to the property itself. The appraisers judged the eleven remaining acres of the Wise farm to be worth $2,500. Adjusted for inflation, the land was worth almost $60,000. It was a form of wealth that Phebe was never able to tap into because of the threat of responsibility and unworthiness driven into her by her father.

Considering that the Great Depression was still devastating the United States in 1933, the estate sale of the stoves and chairs raised only $5.75. After cleaning, some of Phebe's personal property, including rugs and clothes, sold for $35.65. The wood of the house and barn was sold for $100.00. The land proved difficult to sell. Cline attempted to interest buyers, as Phebe's creditors were petitioning him for payment from her estate. In 1937, a creditor petitioned the court to remove Cline as the administrator, but he was finally able to sell the property soon thereafter for $1,240.00. In the end, Phebe's material world was worth not the $100,000 or $1 million of legend but only $1,325.21. That amounted to less than what she owed creditors, resulting in the creditors being paid at only 67 percent the value of their claims.

Christian Wise's valuable spring is now largely ignored, occasionally swam in by Canada geese. As of 2023, the pond is surrounded by a homely orange snow fence, which was presumably placed there for safety purposes, preventing any stray Ohio State Reformatory guests from wandering over and falling in on a ghost tour night or during the Inkcarceration music festival. There is no historical marker present at the pond to tell the story of Louis Bromfield's encounter with Phebe's horse Scottie or how, that day, Phebe designated the boy "a little tetched," so the spring remains, for the time being, beneath the tourist radar.

The flowers that still come up around the long-gone house where Phebe Wise once lived. *Author's collection.*

Reports of ghostly lights around the Wise house in the mid-1930s were most likely later adventurers exploring the abandoned cottage, though tales of a ghostly figure garbed in layers of old-fashioned dresses walking in the area has persistently cropped up over the years, particularly on the road between the reformatory and the old Wise property.

In time, the old house was torn down, leaving little physical trace of Phebe Wise on Hancock Heights—aside from her flowers. But her influence still lingers in the lore of Mansfield and in echoes far beyond.

BIBLIOGRAPHY

Books

Baughman, A.J. *History of Richland County Ohio from 1808 to 1908*. Vol. 2. Chicago: S.J. Clarke Publishing Co., 1908.

Bromfield, Louis. *Animals and Other People*. New York: Harper and Brothers Publishers, 1955.

———. *Awake and Rehearse*. New York: Frederick A. Stokes Company, 1929.

———. *Pleasant Valley*. New York: Harper and Brothers Publishers, 1945.

———. *The Strange Case of Miss Annie Spragg*. New York: Appleton, 1928.

———. *The World We Live In*. New York: Blakiston Company, 1944.

Hazen, Marji. "Phoebe Wise." In *Heritage: People of Richland County*. Vol. 2. Mansfield: Richland County Chapter 70 of the Ohio Genealogical Association, 1966.

The Herald's Directory to Mansfield. Mansfield, OH: *Mansfield Herald*, 1886.

Heyman, Stephen. *The Planter of Modern Life: Louis Bromfield and the Seeds of a Food Revolution*. New York: W.W. Norton and Co., 2020.

Jordan, Mark Sebastian. *The Ceely Rose Murders at Malabar Farm*. Charleston, SC: The History Press, 2021.

———. *Phoebe: A Historical Drama*. Mansfield, OH: Sinister Hand Media, 2005.

Mansfield City Directory. Mansfield, OH: *Mansfield News Journal*, 1920.

Mitchell, Brett. *Life of the Tetched Phoebe Wise*. Mansfield, OH: Historical Preservation, 2004.

Richland County Directory. Mansfield, OH: *Mansfield News*, 1915.

Scott, Ivan. *Louis Bromfield, Novelist and Agrarian Reformer.* Lewiston, NY: Edwin Mellen Press, 1998.

Periodicals

(Note: Variable spellings of names are given as rendered in the original articles.)

Ashland Times Gazette. March 16, 1923.

Bellville Messenger. "Burglars at Work." April 6, 1899, 1.

Cincinnati Enquirer. "Persistent." May 24, 1898, 6.

———. "'Zip' Tyler." December 24, 1891, 10.

Cincinnati Post. "Neighborhood News." April 28, 1892, 2.

Daily Shield and Banner. "'Zip' the Hermit." December 30, 1889.

Detroit Free Press. "State Items." January 16, 1892, 3.

Futty, John. "Tale of Two Cities: The Journey from OSR to ManCI." *Mansfield News Journal*, December 9, 1990.

Hazen, Marji. "Tragic Tale of Phoebe Wise: Woman a Town Scorned." *Mansfield News Journal*, November 7, 1965, 1D.

Jordan, Mark Sebastian. "History Knox: Colorful Figures Loom in Jelloway History." KnoxPages. June 1, 2019. www.knoxpages.com.

———. "History Knox: Old Pharris Played On, Even After Brutal Attack." KnoxPages. February 25, 2023. www.knoxpages.com.

Mansfield Daily Shield. "Killed Kastinowitz." May 13, 1898.

———. "Without Ceremony." May 25, 1898.

Mansfield Herald. "Local Miscellany." October 15, 1885, 3.

———. "Reply." April 22, 1886.

———. "Wanted to Carve." September 18, 1890, 5.

Mansfield News. "Burglars Frightened from Wise Home." November 22, 1911.

———. "Didn't Lose It All." July 19, 1901.

———. "Local Brevities." January 16, 1918.

———. "Local Happenings of 1898." January 1, 1899.

———. "Neighborhood News." May 24, 1900.

———. "Not That It Matters (Not in the Least)." May 20, 1933.

———. "Passing of Scottie." January 31, 1918.

———. "Phoebe Wise Is Seriously Sick." November 29, 1932.

———. "Phoebe Wise Shoots and Kills Jake Kastanowitz." May 22, 1898.

———. "Reports of Death Were Exaggerated." January 14, 1918.

Mansfield News Journal. "Bromfield to Write on Dream Farm Here." November 11, 1938.

———. "Here's Reprint of 'Ballad of Phoebe.'" November 16, 1960, 12.

———. "Last of Her Pets Gone, So She Asks Aid." May 17, 1926, 2.

———. "Mourns Loss of Her Little Pet." May 17, 1926.

———. "Owner Grieving for Scottie, '35' Who Died Today." March 14, 1923.

———. "Phoebe Wise Death Stirs Flood of Reminiscences." March 14, 1933.

———. "Recluse Dies." March 13, 1933.

———. "Robbery Attempt Recalls Legend of Hidden Jewels." January 5, 1931.

———. "Up and Down the Street." November 28, 1940.

———. "Value Phoebe Wise Estate at $1000." April 12, 1933.

———. "Vandals Ransack Old Home of Phoebe Wise in Search of Treasured Trinkets." March 21, 1933.

Mansfield Sunday News. "Taxpayers Whose Personality Is Listed at $3,000 or Over, 1898." July 8, 1888.

Mansfield Weekly News. "Kastinowitz Again." July 14, 1896.

Mattox, Margaret. "Stories of Eccentric Phoebe Wise Linger Among Old-Timers." *Mansfield News Journal*, August 14, 1955, 27.

Narvaja, Norm. "'Phoebe' Comes Back to Life at Malabar Farm." *Mansfield News Journal*, October 7, 2005.

Richland Shield and Banner. "Bothersome Jake." December 21, 1897.

———. "Burglar Killed at Gallipolis." February 6, 1902.

———. "Criminal Assault." August 4, 1894, 7.

———. "Diamond Pin." August 27, 1897, 6.

———. "Gagged and Robbed." December 26, 1891.

———. "Guilty Is the Jury's Verdict." January 10, 1907, 1.

———. "Killed Kastanowitz." May 24, 1898.

———. "A Mere Formality." May 27, 1898.

———. "News of the Week." November 9, 1897, 8.

———. "Pestiferous Jake." November 14, 1896, 7.

———. "Probate Notes." August 5, 1893.

———. "Probate Notes." August 4, 1894.

Schlechty, Jason. "The Baxter Stove Company Comes to Mansfield." Sherman Room at MRCPL. https://theshermanroom.wordpress.com/2020/09/11/the-baxter-stove-company-comes-to-mansfield/.

Scott, Rebecca Chatlain. "Public Letters." *Mansfield News Journal*, November 11, 1965.

Semi Weekly News. "Brief News Notes." June 14, 1895.

———. "Confessed It." December 24, 1895, 6.

———. "Jake at His Old Tricks." November 10, 1896, 4.

———. "Kastinowitz." May 24, 1898.

———. "Kastanowitz Fined." March 27, 1896.

———. "Their Troubles." August 31, 1897, 8.

———. "Very Much Fuss." March 27, 1896, 6.

Stanfield, Virgil A. "The Colorful Personalities in City's History: The Mansfield That Was." *Mansfield News Journal,* April 29, 1973.

———. "Phoebe Becomes County Legend." *Mansfield News Journal,* March 20, 1977, 5C.

Stark County Democrat. "Cullings and Scribblings." November 24, 1881, 8.

Telegraph-Forum. "Local." July 2, 1880, 3.

———. "Local." January 3, 1890, 3.

Weekly News. "Are They the Robbers?" December 24, 1891.

———. "Bound Over to Court." January 1, 1892.

———. "Brief Mention." July 20, 1893.

———. "Brief Mentions." January 7, 1892.

———. "Brief Mentions." April 21, 1892.

———. "Coroner's Finding." June 8, 1905, 12.

———. "Cranky Kastanowitz." August 11, 1892.

———. "Five Go to the Pen." April 28, 1892.

———. "Hunting for Hemp." December 24, 1891.

———. "Landed at the Pen Drunk." May 19, 1892, 8.

———. "Probate Notes." August 10, 1893.

———. "Pursued by a Crank." October 22, 1891.

———. "Those Jail Deliveries." July 28, 1892.

———. "Turn 'Em All Out." November 10, 1892, 2.

———. "Zweifel Guilty." May 19, 1892, 3.

———. "Zweifel's Return." January 14, 1892.

Weekly Register. "Bold Robbers." February 5, 1902, 1.

White, Paul L. "A Glimpse of the Mansfield That Was." *Mansfield News Journal,* February 18, 1968, 5D.

Williams, Jane. "Death Claims Phoebe Wise." *Mansfield News,* March 13, 1933.

———. "20 Years Ago Today." *Mansfield News,* May 14, 1912.

Woodman, D.K. "The Ballad of Phoebe Wise." *Mansfield News Journal,* September 6, 1981.

Interviews

Geld, Ellen Bromfield. Interview with the author. 2005.
Hautzenroeder, Adelia. Correspondence with the author. 2005.
Jackson, Wes. Interview with the author. 2010.
Schroff, Glenn. Interview with the author. 2005.

INDEX

ABOUT THE AUTHOR

Mark Sebastian Jordan is a writer and storyteller who lives in the central highlands of Ohio. His book *The Ceely Rose Murders at Malabar Farm* was published by The History Press in 2021. His column "History Knox" appears weekly on www.KnoxPages.com. Jordan received an Excellence Award from the Ohio Arts Council in 2018 for his music criticism at Seen and Heard International, MusicWeb International, the WordPress blog *Borderlands* and elsewhere. He has written program notes for the Cleveland Orchestra, the Mansfield Symphony, and other musical ensembles, as well as giving extensive music appreciation talks. Widely published as a poet, Jordan was most recently featured in *I Thought I Heard a Cardinal Sing: Ohio's Appalachian Voices*. Also an actor and director for over thirty years, Jordan appeared as an extra in the classic film *The Shawshank Redemption*.

Visit us at
www.historypress.com